Calculator Applications for Business

4th Edition

Sandra Yelverton, Ed.D.
Education Administrator, Retired
Business and Marketing
Alabama Department of Education

SOUTH-WESTERN
CENGAGE Learning

Australia • Brazil • Japan • Korea • Mexico • Singapore • Spain • United Kingdom • United States

Calculator Applications for Business, Fourth Edition

Sandra Yelverton

VP/Editorial Director:
Jack W. Calhoun

VP/Editor-in-Chief:
Karen Schmohe

Acquisitions Editor:
Marilyn Hornsby

Project Manager:
Dr. Inell Bolls

Marketing Manager:
Michael Cloran

Marketing Coordinator:
Georgianna Wright

Senior Production Editor:
Martha Conway

Senior Manufacturing Coordinator:
Charlene Taylor

Production House:
electro-publishing

Art Director:
Tippy McIntosh

Cover and Internal Designer:
Lou Ann Thesing

Cover Images:
© PhotoDisc, Digital Vision

Printer:
Banta Company
Harrisonburg, VA

For more information about our products, contact us at:

South-Western
5191 Natorp Boulevard
Mason, Ohio 45040
USA

ASIA (including India)
Cengage Learning
www.cengageasia.com
tel: (65) 6410 1200

AUSTRALIA/NEW ZEALAND
Cengage Learning
www.cengage.com.au
tel: (61) 3 9685 4111

Represented in Canada by Nelson Education, Ltd.
www.nelson.com
tel: (416) 752 9100 /
     (800) 668 0671

UK/EUROPE/MIDDLE EAST/AFRICA
Cengage Learning
www.cengage.co.uk
tel: (44) 207 067 2500

Contents

Unit 2: Sales, Fund Raising, and Earnings Reports 53

Unit 3: Various Reports, Installment Buying, and Inventory . .105

Acknowledgment

Special thanks to the technical reviewer who performed accuracy checks and provided detailed suggestions in the development of this textbook to ensure that the applications replicate those found in business:

Mark Massen
Massen & Associates Financial Services
Westerville, Ohio

Introduction

Using some form of calculator is not new to you. You may have used a small handheld calculator, a desktop calculator, or a keypad on the computer. You may have used a calculator in your home, in your mathematics classes, and in your business classes. Now you are ready to learn how people use the calculator in business.

The applications in this text-workbook were collected from a variety of businesses: airlines, car rental agencies, service stations, car wash centers, restaurants, banks, bookstores, and many other businesses. As you complete each application, imagine yourself using a ten-key pad on a calculator or computer for the business. You will learn to manage your time, become familiar with business forms, develop accuracy and speed operating the calculator, increase math skills, and explore career opportunities in the fields represented in these applications.

You as a Time Manager

For each application, keep an accurate record of your time. At the top of each application, write the time you start, the time you stop, and the minutes you required to complete the application. If you have not completed an application when a class period ends or time is called, write down the time you stop. Next class, again write down the time you start and the time you finish that same application. Add the minutes you required the first class period to the minutes you required the second class period to obtain the total minutes required. By keeping track of the time you take to complete each application, you will have a record of the total time you take to complete an entire unit. Units 1 and 2 should be completed in approximately 200 minutes, and Units 3 and 4 should be completed in 250 minutes.

You will receive a grade for the time you required to complete each unit correctly. Ask your teacher to approve your unit after you have double-checked each application. Speed and efficiency are important as you complete each unit; however, accuracy will determine your grade. The time you take to correct errors found by your teacher will be added to your record. Thus, your grade may be lowered if you do not seek accuracy as you complete each application. When your teacher has approved a unit, complete the Unit Applications Evaluation for that unit, which should be completed in approximately 50 minutes. If your teacher instructs you to do so, you should then take the Unit Review Test, which should be completed in 50 minutes.

You as a Calculator Operator

As you prepare the applications in this text-workbook, you should:

1. Review the basic calculator operations. Refer to the calculator's operating manual or computer's help menu, or ask your teacher for help with functions that you are unsure of performing. Use proper fingering techniques to develop your speed and accuracy.

2. Listen to your teacher as each unit is explained. Ask questions before you start the unit. You will waste time later if you do not listen.

3. Read and follow instructions carefully for each application. Some applications appear in more than one unit; therefore, be sure to understand and remember instructions for future use.

4. Double-check your work as you go, looking at the tape or printout and comparing what you wanted the calculator to do for you with what the tape/printout shows. If you add a column, compare the column line by line with the column on the tape/printout or complete an activity twice to verify the result.

5. Maintain a positive attitude toward your work. Performing the same calculator operation repeatedly improves speed and accuracy. Every day your goal should be to do your best.

6. Strive to increase your speed while maintaining 100% accuracy on the calculator. Future employers will expect you to make very few errors and to complete your work in a timely manner.

Your Career in Business

The applications in this text-workbook are based on realistic tasks performed by workers in business. Workers in accounting, bookkeeping, or record keeping positions perform each application in this text-workbook. Some applications are used in large corporations, while other applications are used in small offices. As you complete the applications, ask yourself how and why these forms are used in business. Also, ask yourself where the applications are used.

For each application, consider a career in that field by asking yourself these questions:

1. What skills are required for this career field?
2. What school subjects will prepare me for this career field?
3. Will additional training after graduation be needed?
4. What jobs are available in this career field?
5. What are the advancement opportunities in this career field?

You are now ready to begin Unit 1. Read and follow all instructions carefully.

Airline, Stock Portfolio, Auto Cost, and Banking Activities

Name

Date Started

Date Completed

Unit 1 encompasses 16 applications. You should complete the unit in approximately 200 minutes. Read the instructions carefully. If you do not understand an instruction, ask your teacher for help. Decide approximately how much time to spend on each application. Judge your time so you meet the deadline of 200 minutes for the entire unit.

When you start each application, write the time on the form below. When you stop each application, write the time and the number of minutes you required. When you have completed all 16 applications, ask your teacher the procedure for submitting this unit for approval. Do not begin Unit 2 until your teacher has approved Unit 1.

 Unit One Time Record

Application	Time Stopped	Time Started	Minutes Required
1-1			
1-2			
1-3			
1-4			
1-5			
1-6			
1-7			
1-8			
1-9			
1-10			
1-11			
1-12			
1-13			
1-14			
1-15			
1-16			
Total Minutes Required			

Teacher's Approval

3

Application 1-1
Calculate International Flights Boarding Report

OBJECTIVES

Upon completion of this application, you will be able to:

1. Add numbers vertically.
2. Operate a ten-key pad using the touch method.
3. Solve business problems using addition.

INSTRUCTIONS

Add each column down and write the totals.

COASTAL AIRWAYS
WEEKLY INTERNATIONAL FLIGHTS PASSENGER BOARDING REPORT

City _Atlanta_   Week Ending _12/7/--_

Flight	Sunday	Monday	Tuesday	Wednesday	Thursday	Friday	Saturday
16	101	227	97	74	84	231	113
24	112	272	105	83	90	267	123
32	109	198	98	95	67	234	93
40	176	260	86	69	75	241	134
48	96	186	102	81	92	250	93
56	132	251	107	100	116	218	125
64	97	236	99	105	87	271	112
72	85	234	143	112	103	225	126
80	143	243	121	76	231	212	91
88	98	150	89	93	102	137	147
96	224	321	298	275	281	325	279
Total							

Application 1-2

Prepare a First-Quarter Boarding Report

OBJECTIVES

Upon completion of this application, you will be able to:

1. Add and verify whole numbers.
2. Operate a ten-key pad using the touch method.
3. Audit and correct a report.

INSTRUCTIONS

1. Add each column down; verify or correct totals.
2. Add each line across; verify or correct totals.
3. A space is left blank because the current sum of the Total column does not agree with the current sum of the Total line across the bottom. Fill in the correct total.

COASTAL AIRWAYS FIRST-QUARTER PASSENGER BOARDING REPORT

City Atlanta

Quarter Ending 3/31/--

City	January	February	March	Total
Atlantic City, NJ	24,096	19,542	23,847	67,485
Baltimore, MD	13,427	10,261	11,188	34,876
Charleston, SC	6,293	5,037	5,866	17,196
Daytona Beach, FL	39,687	35,274	36,846	110,807
Jacksonville, FL	24,085	35,274	36,846	96,205
Key West, FL	14,599	13,906	15,209	43,714
Melbourne, FL	3,206	2,884	3,505	9,595
Miami, FL	48,397	45,276	47,001	130,674
New Bern, NC	7,291	5,283	6,208	18,782
New Haven, CT	3,826	3,074	3,627	10,527
Newport News, VA	12,005	10,397	11,478	33,880
Norfolk, VA	18,473	16,205	19,036	53,214
Portland, ME	6,405	5,773	6,500	18,678
Presque Isle, ME	7,007	6,029	7,115	20,151
Providence, RI	9,637	7,940	8,356	25,933
Rocky Mount, NC	4,261	3,530	4,006	11,797
Savannah, GA	16,305	15,730	16,502	48,537
St. Simons Island, GA	5,052	5,006	5,124	15,182
Virginia Beach, VA	3,093	2,837	3,115	9,045
Wilmington, NC	8,050	7,265	8,119	23,434
Total	275,195	256,523	279,494	

Application 1-3
Complete an Annual Boarding Report

OBJECTIVES

Upon completion of this application, you will be able to:

1. Add numbers vertically and horizontally.
2. Operate a ten-key pad using the touch method.
3. Solve business problems using addition.

INSTRUCTIONS

1. Add each line across to calculate the annual total for each flight; write the totals.
2. Add each column down to calculate the quarterly totals for all flights; write the totals.
3. Verify that the sum of the Annual Total column matches the sum of the quarterly totals (the bottom row).

COASTAL AIRWAYS ANNUAL PASSENGER BOARDING REPORT

City _Miami, FL_   _Fourth_ Quarter

Flight	1st Quarter Jan.-Mar.	2nd Quarter Apr.-June	3rd Quarter July-Sept.	4th Quarter Oct.-Dec.	Annual Total
109	1,474	1,770	1,918	5,162	
115	1,704	1,978	2,558	6,240	
204	1,887	1,997	2,465	6,349	
228	2,582	2,852	2,910	8,074	
319	2,197	2,558	2,700	7,455	
330	2,445	2,585	2,889	7,919	
355	2,336	2,663	2,906	7,905	
408	1,546	1,879	2,123	5,548	
472	1,447	1,654	1,890	4,982	
500	1,998	2,664	2,885	7,547	
515	1,998	2,556	2,664	7,218	
583	2,356	2,471	2,747	7,574	
681	2,020	2,145	2,669	6,468	
746	2,646	2,887	2,909	8,442	
792	2,232	2,336	2,854	7,422	
833	1,993	1,996	2,556	6,545	
839	1,744	1,857	1,998	5,599	
911	2,885	2,898	2,910	8,693	
964	2,002	2,465	2,669	7,136	
Total					

Application 1-4

Determine Boarding Percentages

OBJECTIVES

Upon completion of this application, you will be able to:

1. Divide whole numbers.

2. Add numbers vertically.

3. Combine division and addition to solve business problems.

4. Solve business problems using percents.

INSTRUCTIONS

1. Calculate the totals of Columns 2 and 3; write the totals at the bottoms of the columns.

2. Set the decimal selector mode at zero. Calculate the percentage of seats sold for each city by inputting the amount in Column 3 then pressing the division key. Input the Column 2 amount and press the percent key or equals sign ("=") on some calculator models.

3. Calculate the Percentage Sold for all cities by repeating Step 2.

COASTAL AIRWAYS BOARDING PERCENTAGE REPORT			
1 City of Departure	2 Seats Available	3 Seats Sold	4 Percentage Sold
Baltimore, MD	38,310	30,265	
Charleston, SC	10,470	7,120	
Daytona Beach, FL	19,530	14,648	
Jacksonville, FL	42,630	41,351	
Key West, FL	16,080	15,758	
Melbourne, FL	5,940	5,287	
Miami, FL	58,920	56,563	
New Bern, NC	28,830	23,929	
New Haven, CT	5,400	4,536	
Newport News, VA	15,540	14,141	
Norfolk, VA	20,610	15,045	
Portland, ME	7,100	5,112	
Presque Isle, ME	8,640	7,344	
Providence, RI	12,840	11,941	
Rocky Mount, NC	5,400	4,644	
St. Simons Island, GA	5,940	5,643	
Savannah, GA	19,530	17,577	
Trenton, NJ	4,860	3,936	
West Palm Beach, FL	29,130	26,800	
Wilmington, NC	10,140	8,923	
Total			

Application 1-5
Calculate Weekly Ticket Sales

Time Stopped _____

– Time Started _____

= Minutes Required _____

OBJECTIVES

Upon completion of this application, you will be able to:

1. Add numbers horizontally.

2. Add numbers vertically.

3. Determine total sales for a week by class of ticket and city.

INSTRUCTIONS

Sales for eight classes of airline tickets to five cities are shown below. Calculate total sales for the week by following these steps:

1. Add each line across; write the total sales for each class of ticket.

2. Add each column down; write the total for each city.

3. Calculate the grand total of sales for the week.

GRAND TIME TRAVEL AGENCY
Airline Weekly Ticket Sales by Class
Week ending 5/20/--

Class of Ticket	San Jose	New York	Dallas	Chicago	Denver	Total
First	3	1	13	6	17	
Coach (flexible)	89	76	34	98	59	
Coach (discounted)	87	32	65	73	53	
Coach (deeply discounted)	34	29	37	27	35	
Business	29	30	17	26	19	
Business Economy	36	27	31	19	25	
Award	10	15	12	14	7	
Special Fares	20	17	14	13	25	
Total						

Application 1-6

Prepare a Weekly Receipts Report

OBJECTIVES

Upon completion of this application, you will be able to:

1. Multiply whole numbers horizontally.
2. Determine a grand total of sales for a week.

INSTRUCTIONS

The fare and number of tickets sold by class for two flights are given below. Calculate the amount sold for each class of ticket, the total number of tickets sold, and the total amount of money collected for those tickets for the week.

1. Multiply the Fare by the Number of Tickets Sold for each class of ticket for Flight #822; write the Amount Sold for each class of ticket.

2. Add the Number of Tickets Sold column for Flight #822; write the subtotal. Add the Amount Sold column for Flight #822; write the subtotal.

3. Complete Steps 1 and 2 for Flight #1037.

4. Add the subtotals; write the totals for the two columns.

COASTAL AIRWAYS WEEKLY RECEIPTS

City __Baltimore__   Week __June 24-30, 20--__

Flight	Class	Fare	Number of Tickets Sold	Amount Sold
822	L	$ 224	10	$
	Q	329	15	
	H	502	20	
	M	717	25	
	Y	1,176	164	
	FIRST	1,576	14	
	Subtotal			$
1037	L	138	19	
	Q	307	25	
	H	468	34	
	M	648	39	
	Y	1,126	225	
	FIRST	1,440	26	
	Subtotal			$
Total				$

MONEY MULTIPLIER CHECKING

Account No. **121-212-8**

Statement Date
July 3, 20--

CAPITAL CITY BANK

Page 2 of 2

QUICK STEPS TO BALANCE YOUR CHECKING ACCOUNT

This form is provided as a service to our customers. Use it to help balance your account.

Statement Ending Balance	$3,192.40	A
Enter total of deposits or credits made but not shown on this statement. *(See worksheet below.)*	+	B
Total lines A and B	=	C
Enter total of checks or other withdrawals made but not shown on this statement. *(See worksheet below.)* −		D
Subtract line D from line C. *This adjusted statement balance should match your checkbook balance.*	=	E

Worksheet

+ List any DEPOSITS or CREDITS which you made that are not shown on this statement.		- List any CHECKS or other WITHDRAWALS which you made that are not shown on this statement.			
Date	Amount	Check #	Amount	Check #	Amount
Total	$		Total	$	
Enter on line B above			Enter on line D above		

Transactions Often Overlooked

+ CREDITS that you may not have entered in your checkbook such as direct deposits of payroll and interest earned.	- WITHDRAWALS that you may not have entered in your checkbook such as bank drafts and loan payments.

Unit 1
Applications Evaluation

Last Name   First Name

Refer to completed Applications 1-1 though 1-16 to answer the following questions. The total point value of all the questions for each application as well as the point value of each individual question is indicated by the numbers in parentheses. Leave the Points Earned column blank. Your teacher will complete it.

Application 1-1

Points Earned

Calculate International Flights Boarding Report

(22) (2 each)

For the week, what was the total number of passengers boarded on

_____
of 22

Flight 16 _____   Flight 24 _____   Flight 32 _____   Flight 40 _____

Flight 48 _____   Flight 56 _____   Flight 64 _____   Flight 72 _____

Flight 80 _____   Flight 88 _____   Flight 96 _____

Application 1-2

Prepare a First-Quarter Boarding Report

(22) (Value beside each)

What was the total number of passengers boarded in

_____
of 22

January (1) _____   February (1) _____   March (1) _____

What was the total number of passengers boarded in all cities for three months?

(1) _____

What was the total number of passengers boarded in all FL, SC, and NC cities in

January (3) _____   February (3) _____   March (3) _____

What was the total number of passengers boarded in all cities except FL, SC, and NC in

January (3) _____   February (3) _____   March (3) _____

Application 1-3

Complete an Annual Boarding Report

(12) (Value beside each)

What was the total number of passengers boarded in the 1st quarter? (1) _____

_____
of 12

What was the total number of passengers boarded in the 2nd quarter? (1) _____

What was the total number of passengers boarded in the 4th quarter? (1) _____

What was the total number of passengers boarded during all quarters on Flights 109, 115, 408, 472, 746, and 792? (3) _____

What was the total number of passengers boarded during all quarters on Flights 204, 228, 500, 515, 583, 911, and 964? (3) _____

What was the total number of passengers boarded during all quarters on Flights 319, 330, 355, 681, 833, and 839? (3) _____

Application 1-4

Determine Boarding Percentages

(12) (Value beside each)

What was the total number of seats available for all cities?	(1) _____
What was the total number of seats sold for all cities?	(1) _____
What was the total percentage sold for all cities?	(1) _____
How many cities had a 95% or greater record?	(2) _____
How many cities had a 90% or greater record?	(2) _____
How many cities had less than the total percentage sold?	(3) _____
Which city had the highest percentage of seats sold?	(1) _____
Which city had the lowest percentage of seats sold?	(1) _____

of 12

Application 1-5

Calculate Weekly Ticket Sales (10) (Value beside each)

What was the total number Coach (deeply discounted) tickets sold?	(1) _____
What was the total number of tickets to Dallas sold?	(1) _____
To which destination were the most tickets sold?	(2) _____
To which destination were the fewest tickets sold?	(2) _____
In what class of ticket were the most tickets sold?	(2) _____
In what class of ticket were the fewest tickets sold?	(2) _____

of 10

Application 1-6

Prepare a Weekly Receipts Report (12) (Value beside each)

What was the total number of tickets sold?	(1) _____
What was the total amount sold?	(1) _____
Which flight had the greatest amount sold?	(2) _____
Between both flights, how many M Class tickets were sold?	(2) _____
How many tickets were sold on Flight 822 in Classes Q, M, and First?	(3) _____
What is the dollar value of the tickets sold on Flight 1037 in Classes L, H and Y?	(3) _____

of 12

Application 1-7

Calculate Daily Seat Availability (16) (2 each)

What was the total number of seats available on the MD80 aircraft?	_____
What was the total number of seats available on the ATR7 aircraft?	_____
What was the total number of seats available on the CRJ aircraft?	_____
What was the total number of seats available on the 757 aircraft?	_____
What was the total number of flights using ATR7s?	_____
What was the total number of flights using CRJs?	_____
What was the total number of flights using 757s?	_____
What was the total number of flights using 767s?	_____

of 16

Application 1-8

Complete a Parking Service Report (5) (1 each)

_____ of 5

What was the total number of tickets sold?

_____

What was the total income?

_____

What was the gate number with the highest Average Ticket Income?

_____

What was the parking lot with the lowest Average Ticket Income?

_____

What was the sum of the Average Ticket Income from all gates and parking lots?

_____

Application 1-9

Determine a Stock Portfolio Valuation (2) (1 each)

_____ of 2

In which corporation was the most money invested?

_____

Which corporation has the highest present value?

_____

Application 1-10

Calculate Yearly Auto Operating Costs (2)

_____ of 2

What is the total of maintenance, gas, and oil for the car costing $29,200?

_____

Application 1-11

Prepare Organization Bank Deposit (2)

_____ of 2

What was the Total Deposit?

_____

Application 1-12

Complete Bank Deposit with Tape/Printout (2)

_____ of 2

What was the Total Deposit?

_____

Application 1-13

Determine a Checkbook Balance (5) (1 each)

_____ of 5

What was the Balance Forward on 6/1?

_____

What was the balance after the 6/1 deposit?

_____

What was the balance after Check No.191 was subtracted?

_____

What was the balance after Check No. 195 was subtracted?

_____

What was the balance on 6/25?

_____

Application 1-14

Prepare a Checkbook Record (8) (Value beside each)

What was the Balance Brought Forward on the Check No. 303 stub?	(1) _____	of 8
What was the Balance after recording the deposit on 3/3?	(1) _____	
To whom was Check No. 318 paid to the order of?	(1) _____	
What was the Balance after subtracting Check No. 321?	(1) _____	
What was the Balance after the ATM cash withdrawal on 3/20?	(1) _____	
What was the total value of Check Nos. 301 through 314 (include 314)?	(3) _____	

Application 1-15

Conduct a Checkbook Register Audit (10) (Value beside each)

What was the Balance after Check No. 624 was subtracted?	(1) _____	of 10
What was the Balance after the 3/1 deposit was added?	(1) _____	
What was the Balance at the end of the Check No. 633 stub?	(1) _____	
For what was Check No. 613 written?	(1) _____	
What was the total amount given in donations?	(2) _____	
What was the total amount spent for groceries?	(2) _____	
What was the total amount spent for rent, city water service, city electric service, and telephone service?	(2) _____	

Application 1-16

Reconcile Bank Statement with Checkbook (8) (1 each)

What was the bank statement balance as of 7/3?	_____	of 8
What was the checkbook register balance before being adjusted?	_____	
What was the total dollar amount of the outstanding checks?	_____	
What was the total dollar amount of ATM withdrawals?	_____	
What was the total dollar amount of POS withdrawals?	_____	
What was the total dollar amount of bank draft withdrawals (include bank loan payments)?	_____	
What was the adjusted checkbook balance?	_____	
What was the adjusted bank statement balance?	_____	

Grading Scale

Total Points Earned of 150   _____

A = 150–139 points
B = 138–128 points
C = 127–117 points
D = 116–106 points

Unit 1 Application Evaluation Grade   _____

Application 2-6
Prepare Earnings Report

OBJECTIVES

Upon completion of this application, you will be able to:

1. Add selected columns horizontally.

2. Add columns vertically.

3. Verify selected totals.

INSTRUCTIONS

Complete the Bookstore Earnings Report as follows:

1. Calculate the Books Sold in each classification for both stores by adding across the figures in Column 1 and Column 3. Write the total of each pair of figures in Column 5. Work across the report line by line.

2. Calculate the Total Sales in each classification for both stores by adding across the figures in Column 2 and Column 4. Write the total of each pair of figures in Column 6. Work across the report line by line.

3. Add all columns to calculate the totals.

4. Verify your calculations. The sum of the totals of Columns 1 and 3 should match the total of Column 5. The sum of the totals of Columns 2 and 4 should match the total of Column 6.

BOOKSTORE EARNINGS REPORT FOR THE MONTH OF *September* 20 --

	1	2		3	4		5	6	
CLASSIFICATION	**Eastside Store**			**Mall Store**			**Both Stores**		
	BOOKS SOLD	TOTAL SALES		BOOKS SOLD	TOTAL SALES		BOOKS SOLD	TOTAL SALES	
Action/Adventure	39	$ 539	60	31	$ 428	91		$	
Art	12	224	98	21	393	71			
Astrology	5	98	50	0	0	00			
Audio	36	368	00	63	644	00			
Biography	28	506	90	38	687	94			
Business	30	238	75	40	319	67			
Classics	10	300	10	16	480	00			
Computers	82	1,226	00	89	1,330	66			
Cooking	74	1,110	00	24	360	00			
Drama	22	270	26	12	319	40			
Entertainment	10	357	99	19	680	01			
Family Care	111	2,226	00	91	1,824	91			
Fantasy	14	209	30	16	239	20			
Fiction	69	1,241	31	79	1,421	21			
Fitness/Nutrition	57	2,137	15	73	2,737	17			
Games	27	339	93	47	591	73			
Gardening	9	194	31	3	64	77			
Hobbies/Crafts	81	157	95	81	157	95			
Home Care	8	220	00	13	357	50			
Languages	4	58	80	0	0	00			
Local Interest	20	279	00	24	334	80			
Magazines	157	392	50	187	467	50			
Medical Care	27	808	65	17	509	15			
Mystery	91	2,528	89	52	1,445	08			
Nature	23	457	70	3	59	70			
New Age	17	424	15	46	1,147	70			
Poetry	40	1,096	00	24	657	60			
Religion/Philosophy	9	314	28	5	177	38			
Relationships	43	1,182	50	47	1,292	50			
Romance	95	1,733	75	115	2,098	75			
Science	39	1,540	50	19	750	50			
Science Fiction	97	1,721	75	79	1,402	25			
Self-Help	104	2,074	80	84	1,675	80			
Social Science	51	966	15	28	530	44			
Sports	94	2,114	06	49	1,102	01			
Study Aids	46	135	70	26	76	70			
Travel	57	1,197	00	75	1,575	00			
True Crime	89	2,843	55	98	3,131	10			
Young Adult Series	37	405	15	16	175	20			
Total		$			$			$	

Application 2-7
Update Inventory Reports

OBJECTIVES

Upon completion of this application, you will be able to:

1. Add numbers horizontally.
2. Add numbers vertically.
3. Update inventory.
4. Verify totals.

INSTRUCTIONS

Complete the Recorded Media Inventory report as follows:

1. Add each row across to obtain the total of each music medium on hand; write the totals.
2. Calculate the inventory by classification by adding each column; write the totals.

3. If the figure for the horizontal final total matches the figure for the vertical final total, place a checkmark beside the total. If the totals do not match, add the figures until you calculate two totals that are the same.

Complete the Miscellaneous Units Inventory report as follows:

1. Add each row across to obtain the total of each miscellaneous unit available for sale; write the totals.
2. Calculate the items on hand 6/12, the items received 6/13, and the items available for sale 6/15 by adding each column; write the totals.
3. If the figure for the horizontal final total matches the figure for the vertical final total, place a checkmark beside the total. If the totals do not match, add the figures until you calculate two totals that are the same.

MERRY MUSIC COMPANY
Recorded Media Inventory

Date *June 15*, 20 --

Recorded Music	Children	Christmas	Classical	Country	Comedy	Easy Listening	Gospel	Jazz	International	Pop	R&B	Rap	Techno	Total
Cassette	23	52	27	62	22	23	34	19	10	187	75	101	10	
CD	25	31	29	77	31	89	76	87	20	251	64	263	12	
VHS	20	35	10	59	12	68	42	23	20	268	36	310	32	
DVD	0	2▣	15	63	20	25	31	46	20	143	29	147	17	
Total														

MERRY MUSIC COMPANY
Miscellaneous Units Inventory

Date *June 15*, 20 --

Miscellaneous Units	On Hand 6/12	Received 6/13	Total Available for Sale 6/15
Apparel	37	50	
Electronic Assessories	52	25	
Novelties	64	40	
Posters	29	30	
Storage	18	25	
Total			

Application 2-8
Determine Average Sales

Time Stopped _____

− Time Started _____

= Minutes Required _____

OBJECTIVES

Upon completion of this application, you will be able to:

1. Determine the average sales made by each branch.

2. Determine the average sales per sales staff.

3. Round numbers.

INSTRUCTIONS

1. For each branch, divide the figure in the Branch Sales column by the number of Sales Staff at that branch. Write the answer in the Average Staff Sales column. Round your answer to two decimal places. The Average Staff Sales for the Quad Cities branch has been calculated for you.

2. Add the Branch Sales column; write the total at the bottom of the column.

3. Add the Sales Staff column; write the total at the bottom of the column.

4. To calculate the Average Staff Sales for all sales staff, divide the total of the Branch Sales column by the total of the Sales Staff column. Round your answer to two decimal places; write your answer in the space at the bottom of the Average Staff Sales column.

5. To calculate the Average Branch Sales, divide the Branch Sales total by the number of branches.

INFORMS BUSINESS FORMS
Branch Sales Week of   May 16, 20--

Branch	City	State	Sales Staff	Branch Sales	Average Staff Sales
Quad Cities	Florence	AL	7	$ 2,354.28	$ 336.33
Sunset	Tucson	AZ	13	3,543.23	
Oceanview	Walnut Creek	CA	9	2,154.89	
Riverside	Denver	CO	16	6,824.72	
Federal Plaza	Washington	DC	11	4,258.92	
Peach Tree	Atlanta	GA	15	4,343.43	
Wheatway	Sioux City	IA	6	1,854.77	
Southland	Baton Rouge	LA	12	4,567.98	
Twin Cities	St. Paul	MN	17	9,876.54	
Red Mountain	Missoula	MT	3	1,052.63	
Woodville	Rural Hill	NC	12	5,231.59	
Central City	Lincoln	NE	11	6,543.21	
Orange Desert	Albuquerque	NM	5	2,458.36	
Pacific Grove	Beaverton	OR	8	7,552.46	
Liberty	Philadelphia	PA	20	8,793.00	
Big Gap	Rapid City	SD	4	1,234.89	
Musicville	Nashville	TN	14	3,522.63	
Astroville	Houston	TX	19	7,000.89	
Tides Town	Virginia Beach	VA	13	5,432.11	
Mine Towne	Charleston	WV	2	1,036.75	
Total				$	$

Average Branch Sales $ _____

Application 2-9
Compute Profit

OBJECTIVES

Upon completion of this application, you will be able to:

1. Determine cost of inventory.
2. Calculate sales income.
3. Compute profit.

INSTRUCTIONS

To complete the Quarterly Sales and Profit Report, follow these steps:

1. For each shoe type, multiply the No. of Pairs Purchased by the Wholesale Price. Record the result in the Cost of Inventory column.

2. Multiply the No. of Pairs Sold by the Retail Price. Record the result in the Sales Income column.

3. To determine the Net Profit on each shoe type, subtract the Cost of Inventory from the Sales Income. Record the difference in the Net Profit column.

4. Total the Cost of Inventory and Sales Income columns. Record the totals at the bottom of the columns.

5. Calculate the quarterly profit by subtracting the Total Cost of Inventory from the Total Sales Income. Record the result at the bottom of the Net Profit column.

CHAMPION QUICKSTART SHOES
Quarterly Sales and Profit Report   Quarter Jan.-Mar. 20--

Shoe Type	No. of Pairs Purchased	Wholesale Price	Cost of Inventory	No. of Pairs Sold	Retail Price	Sales Income	Net Profit
Basketball	40	$ 32.50	$	23	$ 64.99	$	$
Casual	17	15.00		13	29.99		
Crosstrainer	28	30.00		27	59.99		
Fitness	30	23.50		29	46.99		
Golf	72	40.00		61	79.99		
Running	50	27.50		42	54.99		
Soccer Cleats	55	22.50		35	44.99		
Tennis	35	20.00		28	39.99		
Walking	25	17.50		16	34.99		
Total			$			$	$

Application 2-10
Complete Guest Checks and Prepare Report

OBJECTIVES

Upon completion of this application, you will be able to:

1. Verify menu prices.
2. Determine sales tax using a sales tax chart.
3. Add sales receipts and transfer data to a daily report.
4. Prepare a daily report of sales.
5. Calculate an average.

INSTRUCTIONS

Complete each Guest Check as follows:

1. Compare the prices written on each Guest Check with the prices shown on the menu. If you find an error, draw a line through the incorrect figure on the Guest Check and write the correct price nearby.

2. Calculate the total value of the food ordered on each Guest Check; write the figure on the Subtotal line.

3. Determine the tax using the State Sales Tax Chart; write the figure on the Guest Check on the Tax line.

4. Add the Subtotal and Tax figures; write the Total.

Complete the Daily Report for Server 18 as follows:

1. From each Guest Check, transfer the check number, number of persons, food value, tax, and total to the proper columns on the Daily Report.

2. Calculate the totals of the columns.

3. Calculate the Average Check Income by dividing the total amount collected from food (including tax) by the number of Guest Checks.

Quality Cuisine Restaurant

Appetizers & Snacks

EGG ROLLS-Stuffed with shrimp and oriental vegetables $3.49

CHIPS-Crunchy tortilla chips with salsa $1.69

GUACAMOLE-Made fresh from select avocados and served in a tortilla bowl with salsa and sour cream $4.49

POTATO SKINS-With sour cream, bacon, scallions, and cheddar cheese $4.95

NACHOS-
Cheese & jalapenos $2.99
Chili, cheese, & jalapenos $3.99
With fresh guacamole and sour cream, add 99¢

BREADED CHEESE-Deep fried to a crisp golden brown outside, soft and warm inside $4.99

SPICY CATFISH FINGERS- Mild fillets breaded with Cajun seasonings and deep fried $4.95

CHICKEN FINGERS-Tender all-breast chicken, breaded and deep fried $4.99

SAMPLER-Chicken fingers, potato skins, and breaded cheese $6.99

Soups & Salads

SALAD EXTRAVAGANZA
The best salad bar in town. Crisp salad greens, garden-fresh vegetables, creamy salads, croutons, meats, cheeses, and more, plus a choice of dressings

SALAD BAR $3.95
With any food item except side dishes $2.49

*CHICKEN SALAD PLATTER Served with vegetable salad $5.99

*SHRIMP SALAD PLATTER Served with vegetable salad $5.99

FRENCH ONION SOUP With croutons and provolone cheese browned to golden perfection
Cup-$1.99   Bowl-$2.99

SOUP OF THE DAY
Cup-$1.99   Bowl-$2.99

GUMBO
A spicy soup made with shrimp, chicken, sausage, okra, rice, and bayou magic
Cup-$1.99   Bowl-$2.99

Stuffed Potatoes

ALL-AMERICAN-Butter, sour cream, bacon, scallions, and cheddar cheese $3.49

MOTHER LODE-Butter, sour cream, ham, spicy cheese sauce, and scallions $3.49

POTATO AND SALAD OR SOUP-Choice of stuffed potato and salad bar or bowl of soup $5.48

Pasta

A large portion served with garlic bread

LASAGNA-Italian sausage, cheese, and tomato marinara sauce $6.99

SPINACH LASAGNA-A blend of ricotta, provolone, and parmesan cheeses and rich marinara sauce $6.99

Winning Combinations

SOUP AND SALAD BAR $5.48
Choice of soup and salad bar

SOUP AND QUICHE $5.48
Choice of soup and quiche of the day

SALAD BAR AND QUICHE $5.48
Salad bar and quiche of the day

Sandwiches

French fries, add 99¢
Salad bar, add $2.49

FAJITA STEAK SANDWICH Sizzling steak strips with grilled onions and peppers on a whole wheat bun $6.99

ROAST BEEF & MELTED CHEDDAR CROISSANT $5.99

TUNA SALAD CROISSANT Tender chunks of tuna blended with mayonnaise and seasonings $5.99

CROISSANT LE CLUB Ham, roast beef, cheddar, and bacon $5.99

SHRIMP SALAD CROISSANT Sweet and flavorful shrimp, seasoned just right and blended with mayonnaise $5.99

CHEDDAR MELT TRIO Chicken salad or shrimp salad on an English muffin, topped with melted cheddar $4.99
May be served with small salad and no bread

*Low Carb Item

Chicken Sandwiches

Chicken sandwiches are made with only the best natural, whole, boneless chicken breasts. All are served on toasted whole wheat buns.

French fries, add 99¢
Salad bar, add $2.49

SUPER CHICKEN-Charbroiled and topped with ham, cheese, and bacon $5.29

CAJUN-Dipped in Cajun spices, then charbroiled. Served with lettuce, tomato, and Cajun sauce $5.29

TERIYAKI-Marinated, then charbroiled. Served topped with grilled onions and pineapple and covered with melted provolone cheese $5.29

CALIFORNIA-Gilled and topped with sour cream, guacamole, and sprouts $5.29

BBQ-Charbroiled with a distinctive mesquite barbecue sauce, then topped with coleslaw, Southern style $5.29

Chicken Club-Lightly battered and fried, then layered with bacon, lettuce, tomato, and house dressing $5.29

BACON-CHEESE-Lightly battered and fried, then topped with bacon and cheddar cheese $5.29

SMOTHERED-Lightly battered and fried, then smothered with sauteed onions and mushrooms and finished with melted provolone $5.29

PARMESAN-Lightly battered and fried, then topped with marinara sauce, parmesan, and melted provolone $5.29

Chicken

LIGHT FRIED CHICKEN
Marinated in ranch-style seasonings, then lightly breaded and fried. Served with a spicy sauce $9.99

CHICKEN TERIYAKI
Marinated and charbroiled $9.99

SPICY CAJUN CHICKEN
Coated with lively Cajun seasonings and charbroiled $9.99

Entree served with salad and baked beans

Steak

STEAK TERIYAKI
Marinated for flavor and tenderness then charbroiled 7 ounces $8.99

NEW YORK STRIP
A 12-ounce choice cut, grilled to perfection $12.99

BLACKENED NEW YORK STRIP
12 ounces, coated with fiery Cajun spices, then seared in a cast iron skillet $12.99

Entree served with salad and baked potato

Platters

Served with fries and freshly made coleslaw

CHICKEN TERIYAKI	$6.29
BARBECUED CHICKEN	$6.29
CAJUN CHICKEN	$6.29
LEMON CHICKEN FINGERS	$6.29
SPICY CAJUN CATFISH	$5.99
BLACKENED FISH	$6.49

*FIT 'N TRIM PLATTERS
Substitute broccoli and a sprout salad for fries and coleslaw
Priced the same

Burgers

Eight ounces of 100% choice beef. Choose from a variety of toppings. Served on a whole wheat bun (English muffin on request).

French fries, add 99¢
Salad bar, add $2.49

WESTERN-With lettuce, tomato and onion $4.69

FRENCH-With savory mushroom-wine sauce $4.69

ELLERY QUEEN-Plenty of sauteed onions $4.69

Desserts

Our desserts are made in our own kitchen

Icebox Pies-Chocolate, lemon, etc.	$2.40
Homemade Cobbler or Pudding	$1.25
Strawberry Shortcake	$2.50
Hot Fudge Cake	$2.75
Ice Cream, dish	$1.60
Nut Sundae	$2.10
Banana Split	$3.25

Beverages

Coffee	$.89
Milk, homogenized	$.70
Country Fresh Buttermilk	$.70
Root Beer	$.89
Iced Tea	$.89
Cola	$.89
Chocolate Milk	$.70
Hot Chocolate	$.70
Thick Milk Shakes	$1.75
Thick Malted Milk	$1.60

STATE 6% SALES TAX CHART
Combining Local Tax (1$\frac{1}{2}$%) and State Tax (4$\frac{1}{2}$%) = Total (6%)

SALES			SALES		
From	To	Tax	From	To	Tax
0.01	0.10	0.00	9.92	10.08	.60
.11	.24	.01	10.09	10.24	.61
.25	.41	.02	10.25	10.41	.62
.42	.58	.03	10.42	10.58	.63
.59	.74	.04	10.59	10.74	.64
.75	.91	.05	10.75	10.91	.65
.92	1.08	.06	10.92	11.08	.66
1.09	1.24	.07	11.09	11.24	.67
1.25	1.41	.08	11.25	11.41	.68
1.42	1.58	.09	11.42	11.58	.69
1.59	1.74	.10	11.59	11.74	.70
1.75	1.91	.11	11.75	11.91	.71
1.92	2.08	.12	11.92	12.08	.72
2.09	2.24	.13	12.09	12.24	.73
2.25	2.41	.14	12.25	12.41	.74
2.42	2.58	.15	12.42	12.58	.75
2.59	2.74	.16	12.59	12.74	.76
2.75	2.91	.17	12.75	12.91	.77
2.92	3.08	.18	12.92	13.08	.78
3.09	3.24	.19	13.09	13.24	.79
3.25	3.41	.20	13.25	13.41	.80
3.42	3.58	.21	13.42	13.58	.81
3.59	3.74	.22	13.59	13.74	.82
3.75	3.91	.23	13.75	13.91	.83
3.92	4.08	.24	13.92	14.08	.84
4.09	4.24	.25	14.09	14.24	.85
4.25	4.41	.26	14.25	14.41	.86
4.42	4.58	.27	14.42	14.58	.87
4.59	4.74	.28	14.59	14.74	.88
4.75	4.91	.29	14.75	14.91	.89
4.92	5.08	.30	14.92	15.08	.90
5.09	5.24	.31	15.09	15.24	.91
5.25	5.41	.32	15.25	15.41	.92
5.42	5.58	.33	15.42	15.58	.93
5.59	5.74	.34	15.59	15.74	.94
5.75	5.91	.35	15.75	15.91	.95
5.92	6.08	.36	15.92	16.08	.96
6.09	6.24	.37	16.09	16.24	.97
6.25	6.41	.38	16.25	16.41	.98
6.42	6.58	.39	16.42	16.58	.99
6.59	6.74	.40	16.59	16.74	1.00
6.75	6.91	.41	16.75	16.91	1.01
6.92	7.08	.42	16.92	17.08	1.02
7.09	7.24	.43	17.09	17.24	1.03
7.25	7.41	.44	17.25	17.41	1.04
7.42	7.58	.45	17.42	17.58	1.05
7.59	7.74	.46	17.59	17.74	1.06
7.75	7.91	.47	17.75	17.91	1.07
7.92	8.08	.48	17.92	18.08	1.08
8.09	8.24	.49	18.09	18.24	1.09
8.25	8.41	.50	18.25	18.41	1.10
8.42	8.58	.51	18.42	18.58	1.11
8.59	8.74	.52	18.59	18.74	1.12
8.75	8.91	.53	18.75	18.91	1.13
8.92	9.08	.54	18.92	19.08	1.14
9.09	9.24	.55	19.09	19.24	1.15
9.25	9.41	.56	19.25	19.41	1.16
9.42	9.58	.57	19.42	19.58	1.17
9.59	9.74	.58	19.59	19.74	1.18
9.75	9.91	.59			

For amounts above 19.74, multiply the amount of the Guest Check by .06.

Guest Check

Table No.	No. Persons	Server No.	Check No.
4	2	18	**102801**

Roast Beef/Melted Ch.	5	99
French burger	4	69
French fries		99
2 Root Beers @ .89	1	78
SUBTOTAL		
TAX		
THANK YOU! **TOTAL**		

Guest Check

Table No.	No. Persons	Server No.	Check No.
6	3	18	**102802**

Chicken Salad Platter	5	99
Steak Teriyaki	8	99
Blackened Fish Plat.	6	49
3 Coffees @ .89	2	67
Ice cream	1	60
Lemon Icebox Pie	2	45
Cobbler	1	25
SUBTOTAL		
TAX		
THANK YOU! **TOTAL**		

Guest Check

Table No.	No. Persons	Server No.	Check No.
4	1	18	**102803**

Lasagna	6	99
Cola		89
Hot Fudge Cake	2	75
SUBTOTAL		
TAX		
THANK YOU! **TOTAL**		

Guest Check

Table No.	No. Persons	Server No.	Check No.
5	3	18	**102804**

Bacon - Cheese	5	29
Chicken Club	5	29
Western	4	69
Chocolate Shake	1	75
Chocolate Malt	1	60
2 Milks @ .70	1	40
SUBTOTAL		
TAX		
THANK YOU! **TOTAL**		

Guest Check

Table No.	No. Persons	Server No.	Check No.
5	2	18	**102805**

Spicy Cajun Chicken	9	99
Blackened NY Strip	12	99
French Onion Soup Cup	1	99
2 Iced Teas @ .89	1	78
Hot Fudge Cake	2	75
Str. Shortcake	2	50
SUBTOTAL		
TAX		
THANK YOU! **TOTAL**		

Guest Check

Table No.	No. Persons	Server No.	Check No.
4	2	18	**102806**

Croissant le Club	5	99
Blackened NY Strip	12	99
Fries		99
Coffee		89
Iced Tea		89
Chocolate Pie	2	40
Ice Cream	1	60
SUBTOTAL		
TAX		
THANK YOU! **TOTAL**		

Guest Check

Table No.	No. Persons	Server No.	Check No.
6	2	18	**102807**

Ellery Queen	4	69
Western	4	69
2 fries @ .99	1	98
2 Root Beers @ .89	1	78
2 Nut Sundaes @ 2.10	4	20
SUBTOTAL		
TAX		
THANK YOU! **TOTAL**		

Guest Check

Table No.	No. Persons	Server No.	Check No.
6	1	18	**102808**

NY Strip	12	99
Gumbo Cup	1	99
Coffee		89
Hot Fudge Cake	2	75
SUBTOTAL		
TAX		
THANK YOU! **TOTAL**		

Guest Check

Table No.	No. Persons	Server No.	Check No.
6	2	18	**102809**

Spicy Cajun Catfish	5	99
Steak Teriyaki	8	99
Soup of Day Cup	1	99
Salad Bar	2	49
2 Coffees @ .89	1	78
Hot Fudge Cake	2	75
SUBTOTAL		
TAX		
THANK YOU! TOTAL		

Guest Check

Table No.	No. Persons	Server No.	Check No.
4	1	18	**102810**

Fajita Steak Sand.	6	99
Mother Lode Potato	3	49
Coffee		89
Cobbler	1	25
SUBTOTAL		
TAX		
THANK YOU! TOTAL		

Guest Check

Table No.	No. Persons	Server No.	Check No.
4	3	18	**102811**

California	5	29
Chicken Club	5	29
BBQ	5	29
2 All-American @ 3.49	6	98
Choc Malt	1	60
Root Beer		89
Buttermilk		70
SUBTOTAL		
TAX		
THANK YOU! TOTAL		

Guest Check

Table No.	No. Persons	Server No.	Check No.
5	1	18	**102812**

Western	4	69
Salad Bar	2	49
Root Beer		89
Banana Split	3	25
SUBTOTAL		
TAX		
THANK YOU! TOTAL		

Guest Check

Table No.	No. Persons	Server No.	Check No.	
6	3	18	**102813**	
Croissant le Club			5	99
Salad Bar			2	49
Sampler			6	99
2 Iced Teas @ .89			1	78
Milk				70
	SUBTOTAL			
		TAX		
THANK YOU!		TOTAL		

Guest Check

Table No.	No. Persons	Server No.	Check No.	
5	4	18	**102814**	
Shrimp Salad Platter			5	99
Fajita Steak Sand.			6	99
French Burger			4	69
Breaded Cheese			4	99
4 Coffees @ .89			3	56
2 Ice creams @ 1.60			3	20
1 Choc. Pie			2	40
Str. Shortcake			2	50
	SUBTOTAL			
		TAX		
THANK YOU!		TOTAL		

Guest Check

Table No.	No. Persons	Server No.	Check No.	
4	2	18	**102815**	
Ellery Queen Burg.			4	69
French Onion Soup Cup			1	99
B.B.Q.			5	29
Milk Shake			1	75
Root Beer				89
Lemon Pie			2	40
Hot Fudge Cake			2	75
	SUBTOTAL			
		TAX		
THANK YOU!		TOTAL		

Guest Check

Table No.	No. Persons	Server No.	Check No.	
5	1	18	**102816**	
Tuna Sal. Croissant			5	99
Fries				99
Choc. Malt			1	60
Nut Sundae			3	25
	SUBTOTAL			
		TAX		
THANK YOU!		TOTAL		

Guest Check

Table No.	No. Persons	Server No.	Check No.
4	3	18	**102817**

Cheddar Melt Trio	4	99
Western	4	69
Roast Beef/Melted Ch.	5	99
Banana Split	3	25
2 Colas @ .89	1	78
1 Coffee		89
SUBTOTAL		
TAX		
THANK YOU! **TOTAL**		

Guest Check

Table No.	No. Persons	Server No.	Check No.
4	2	18	**102818**

Steak Teriyaki	8	99
Fries		99
Blackened Fish	6	49
Salad Bar	2	49
2 Coffees @ .89	1	78
2 Nut Sundaes @ 2.10	4	20
SUBTOTAL		
TAX		
THANK YOU! **TOTAL**		

Guest Check

Table No.	No. Persons	Server No.	Check No.
4	2	18	**102819**

NY Strip	12	99
Salad Bar	2	49
Cola		89
Iced Tea		89
SUBTOTAL		
TAX		
THANK YOU! **TOTAL**		

Guest Check

Table No.	No. Persons	Server No.	Check No.
6	3	18	**102820**

Super Chicken Sand.	5	29
Bacon Cheese Sand.	5	29
Croissant le Club	5	99
Root Beer		89
Coffee		89
Choc. Milk		70
SUBTOTAL		
TAX		
THANK YOU! **TOTAL**		

Daily Report for Server _18_

Check Number	No. of Persons	Food	Tax	Total
Total				

	Average Check Income	

Application 2-11
Prepare Order Forms

OBJECTIVES

Upon completion of this application, you will be able to:

1. Read a price list and calculate taxes.

2. Complete customer order forms.

3. Transfer totals from completed customer order forms to a daily report.

4. Prepare a daily report.

INSTRUCTIONS

The Price List includes prices for impression printing on one side or two sides of a sheet of paper. At the bottom of the Price List are prices for orders on special paper.

The following examples may aid you in using the Price List:

Example A: 700 copies, two color, 1 side.

In the Quantity column, locate 700; read across to the two color, 1 side column. Write the price of 35.43 on the order form in the Amount column opposite the description.

Example B: 1,400 copies, black, 2 sides.

In the Quantity column, locate 1,000; read across to the black, 2 sides column. The price of 1,000 copies is 63.84. To determine the price of the remaining 400 copies ordered, read down the same column (black, 2 sides) to the Add'l 100s figure. The price for 100 is 9.35; multiply 9.35 by 4 to obtain 37.40, the price for 400 additional copies. Add 63.84 (price for 1000) and 37.40 (price for 400) to obtain 101.24, the price for 1,400 copies. Write the price of 101.24 on the order form in the Amount column opposite the description.

Example C: 1,200 copies, three color, 1 side on colored bond 20#.

In the Quantity column, locate 1,000; read across to the three color, 1 side column. The price for 1,000 copies is 52.10. To determine the price for the remaining 200 copies, read down the same column (three color, 1 side) to the Add'l 100s figure. The price for 100 is 4.70; multiply 4.70 by 2 to obtain 9.40, the price for 200 additional copies. Add 52.10 (price for 1,000) and 9.40 (price for 200) to obtain 61.50, the price of 1,200 copies. Write the price of 61.50 on the order form in the Amount column opposite the description. To determine the price for the special paper, locate at the bottom of the Price List the add 20% for colored bond 20# paper. Multiply 61.50, the price of the 1,200 copies, by 20% to obtain 12.30. Write the price of 12.30 on the order form in the Price column opposite the second line of the description.

To complete the order forms:

1. Determine the price for each order on the order forms by following the procedures given above.

2. Calculate other services of drilling, folding, and stapling and write the figure on the order form in the Amount column opposite the description.

3. Add all figures in the Amount and Price columns; write the figure on the Subtotal line.

4. Multiply the Subtotal by 5% (.05); write the figure on the Tax line.

5. Add the Subtotal and Tax figures; write the Total.

To complete the Daily Report, transfer from each order form the information needed on the Daily Report: Order Number, Subtotal Amount, Tax Charged, and Total Amount. When you have transferred all the data, calculate the totals of the columns.

PRICE LIST

Quantity	Black 1 Side	Black 2 Sides	Two Color 1 Side	Two Color 2 Sides	Three Color 1 Side	Three Color 2 Sides
25	17.86	33.39	18.04	33.62	18.36	34.02
50	18.37	34.17	18.68	34.53	19.22	35.16
75	18.86	34.93	19.31	35.43	20.06	36.28
100	19.37	35.71	19.94	36.34	20.93	37.42
125	19.86	36.47	20.57	37.24	21.78	38.53
150	20.37	37.25	21.21	38.15	22.65	39.66
175	20.88	38.03	21.84	39.03	23.50	40.79
200	21.38	38.80	22.48	39.94	24.37	41.92
225	21.88	39.58	23.11	40.85	25.21	43.06
250	22.38	40.34	23.75	41.75	26.07	44.18
275	22.88	41.12	24.36	42.66	26.93	45.30
300	23.38	41.88	25.00	43.56	27.79	46.43
325	23.89	42.67	25.63	44.47	28.65	47.56
350	24.40	43.44	26.27	45.37	29.51	48.69
375	24.89	44.21	26.90	46.27	30.35	49.82
400	25.40	44.98	27.54	47.17	31.22	50.95
425	25.89	45.75	28.17	48.08	32.07	52.07
450	26.40	46.52	28.81	48.98	32.94	53.19
475	26.89	47.29	29.43	49.89	33.79	54.33
500	27.41	48.08	30.07	50.80	34.66	55.46
525	27.91	48.85	30.70	51.70	35.50	56.59
550	28.41	49.62	31.34	52.59	36.36	57.72
575	28.91	50.39	31.97	53.49	37.22	58.85
600	29.41	51.16	32.61	54.40	38.08	59.97
625	29.91	51.93	33.24	55.30	38.94	61.09
650	30.71	53.01	34.16	56.52	40.10	62.54
675	31.23	53.79	34.80	57.42	40.95	63.66
700	31.73	54.57	35.43	58.33	41.81	64.80
725	32.23	55.33	36.07	59.22	42.67	65.92
750	32.73	56.11	36.70	60.13	43.53	67.04
775	33.23	56.87	37.34	61.03	44.39	68.17
800	33.73	57.65	37.97	61.94	45.25	69.30
825	34.25	58.44	38.60	62.85	46.10	70.44
850	34.74	59.20	39.23	63.75	46.95	71.56
875	35.25	59.98	39.87	64.66	47.82	72.70
900	35.74	60.74	40.50	65.54	48.67	73.81
925	36.25	61.52	41.14	66.45	49.54	74.94
950	36.74	62.28	41.77	67.35	50.39	76.07
975	37.25	63.06	42.41	68.26	51.24	77.20
1,000	37.76	63.84	43.02	69.16	52.10	78.33
Add'l 100s	7.15	9.35	6.85	11.50	4.70	7.75

Special Paper Orders: Colored Bond   20#, add 20%   25# Rag, add 15%
                                       67#, add 30%   Textured, add 35%
                                       70#, add 25%   NCR, add 50%

PRONTO PRINT PLACE

7359 Independence Boulevard
Salt Lake City, UT 84116

Phone: 555-0188
Fax: 555-0189
E-mail: prontoprint@aol.com

Customer Order No. _127_ Date _4/20_ 20 _--_

Name _C & W Enterprises, Inc._ Phone _555-0101_

Address _P. O. Box 2942, Kaysville, UT 84037-2645_

Sold By _12_	Cash	C.O.D.	Charge ✓	On Acct.	Mdse. Retd.	Paid Out	
Quantity	Description				Price	Amount	
875	Black, one side						
50	Black, two sides						
375	Two color, one side						
100	Two color, two sides						
75	Three color, one side						
	Thank You						
	For Your Business						
	Please Come Again!						
					Subtotal		
					Tax		
					Total		

PRONTO PRINT PLACE

7359 Independence Boulevard
Salt Lake City, UT 84116

Phone: 555-0188
Fax: 555-0189
E-mail: prontoprint@aol.com

Customer Order No. _128_ Date _4/20_ 20 _--_

Name _Travis High School_ Phone _555-0198_

Address _3652 Limerick St., Salt Lake City, UT 84121-7921_

Sold By _12_	Cash ✓	C.O.D.	Charge	On Acct.	Mdse. Retd.	Paid Out	
Quantity	Description				Price	Amount	
175	Black, one side						
900	Black, two sides						
125	Two color, two sides						
50	Three color, one side						
100	Three color, two sides						
1,400	Drilled @ .005/sheet						
	Thank You						
	For Your Business						
	Please Come Again!						
					Subtotal		
					Tax		
					Total		

PRONTO PRINT PLACE

7359 Independence Boulevard
Salt Lake City, UT 84116

Phone: 555-0188
Fax: 555-0189
E-mail: prontoprint@aol.com

Customer Order No. _129_   Date _4/20_ 20 _--_

Name _Layton Chamber of Commerce_   Phone _555-0131_

Address _P. O. Box 1000, Layton, UT 84041-6510_

Sold By 6	Cash	C.O.D.	Charge ✓	On Acct.	Mdse. Retd.	Paid Out	
Quantity	Description				Price	Amount	
775	Black, 2 sides						
300	Two color, 1 side						
50	Two color, 2 sides						
550	Three color, 1 side						
125	Three color, 2 sides						
	Thank You						
	For Your Business						
	Please Come Again!						
					Subtotal		
					Tax		
					Total		

PRONTO PRINT PLACE

7359 Independence Boulevard
Salt Lake City, UT 84116

Phone: 555-0188
Fax: 555-0189
E-mail: prontoprint@aol.com

Customer Order No. _130_   Date _4/20_ 20 _--_

Name _Oliver and Ivey_   Phone _555-0144_

Address _Ivey Building, Salt Lake City, UT 85111-7651_

Sold By 6	Cash	C.O.D.	Charge ✓	On Acct.	Mdse. Retd.	Paid Out	
Quantity	Description				Price	Amount	
800	Black, 1 side						
650	Two color, 1 side						
75	Two color, 2 sides						
125	Three color, 1 side						
50	Three color, 2 sides						
650	Folded @ .005/sheet						
	Thank You						
	For Your Business						
	Please Come Again!						
					Subtotal		
					Tax		
					Total		

PRONTO PRINT PLACE

7359 Independence Boulevard
Salt Lake City, UT 84116

Phone: 555-0188
Fax: 555-0189
E-mail: prontoprint@aol.com

Customer Order No. 131   Date 4/20   20 --

Name: Rebecca Cardello, CPA   Phone: 555-0125

Address: 1920 West Olney St., Centerville, UT 84014-3675

Sold By 12	Cash	C.O.D.	Charge ✓	On Acct.	Mdse. Retd.	Paid Out	
Quantity	Description				Price	Amount	
1,300	Black, one side						
475	Two color, two sides						
	on colored bond 67#						
125	Three color, one side						
1,900	Folded @ .005/sheet						
	Thank You						
	For Your Business						
	Please Come Again!						
					Subtotal		
					Tax		
					Total		

PRONTO PRINT PLACE

7359 Independence Boulevard
Salt Lake City, UT 84116

Phone: 555-0188
Fax: 555-0189
E-mail: prontoprint@aol.com

Customer Order No. 132   Date 4/20   20 --

Name: Lockhurst Engineering Corp.   Phone: 555-0150

Address: 404 West Wyler St., Salt Lake City, UT 84109-3621

Sold By 12	Cash ✓	C.O.D.	Charge	On Acct.	Mdse. Retd.	Paid Out	
Quantity	Description				Price	Amount	
50	Black, one side						
	on textured						
600	Black, two sides						
	on colored bond 20#						
125	Three color, two sides						
	Thank You						
	For Your Business						
	Please Come Again!						
					Subtotal		
					Tax		
					Total		

PRONTO PRINT PLACE

7359 Independence Boulevard
Salt Lake City, UT 84116

Phone: 555-0188
Fax: 555-0189
E-mail: prontoprint@aol.com

Customer Order No. _133_   Date _4/20_ 20 _--_

Name _R.L. Mason and Sons_   Phone _555-0180_

Address _P.O. Box 25, Bountiful, UT 84010-9568_

Sold By 6	Cash	C.O.D.	Charge ✓	On Acct.	Mdse. Retd.	Paid Out	
Quantity	Description				Price	Amount	
350	Two color, 1 side						
	on 25# rag						
175	Two color, 2 sides						
	on colored bond 20#						
900	Three color, 2 sides						
	Thank You						
	For Your Business						
	Please Come Again!						
					Subtotal		
					Tax		
					Total		

PRONTO PRINT PLACE

7359 Independence Boulevard
Salt Lake City, UT 84116

Phone: 555-0188
Fax: 555-0189
E-mail: prontoprint@aol.com

Customer Order No. _134_   Date _4/20_ 20 _--_

Name _Clarke Brothers, Inc._   Phone _555-0122_

Address _935 11th Ave., Magna, UT 84044-2732_

Sold By 6	Cash	C.O.D.	Charge ✓	On Acct.	Mdse. Retd.	Paid Out	
Quantity	Description				Price	Amount	
1,500	Black, 1 side						
800	Two color, 2 sides						
	on 25# rag						
625	Three color, 1 side						
	on colored bond 70#						
	Thank You						
	For Your Business						
	Please Come Again!						
					Subtotal		
					Tax		
					Total		

PRONTO PRINT PLACE

7359 Independence Boulevard
Salt Lake City, UT 84116

Phone: 555-0188
Fax: 555-0189
E-mail: prontoprint@aol.com

Customer Order No. _135_   Date _4/20_ 20 _--_

Name _Rich's, Inc._   Phone _555-0199_

Address _847 William Rich Bldg., Salt Lake City, UT 84119-9654_

Sold By 12	Cash	C.O.D.	Charge ✓	On Acct.	Mdse. Retd.	Paid Out	
Quantity	Description				Price	Amount	
275	Two color, two sides on NCR						
1,700	Three color, one side on textured						
275	Drilled @ .005/sheet						
	Thank You						
	For Your Business						
	Please Come Again!						
					Subtotal		
					Tax		
					Total		

PRONTO PRINT PLACE

7359 Independence Boulevard
Salt Lake City, UT 84116

Phone: 555-0188
Fax: 555-0189
E-mail: prontoprint@aol.com

Customer Order No. _136_   Date _4/20_ 20 _--_

Name _Dale Howard Corp._   Phone _555-0167_

Address _2359 South Gaston St., Salt Lake City, UT 84120-9730_

Sold By 12	Cash	C.O.D.	Charge ✓	On Acct.	Mdse. Retd.	Paid Out	
Quantity	Description				Price	Amount	
1,500	Black, two sides on colored bond 70#						
475	Two color, one side on colored bond 67#						
500	Stapled left corner @ .01/staple						
	Thank You						
	For Your Business						
	Please Come Again!						
					Subtotal		
					Tax		
					Total		

PRONTO PRINT PLACE

7359 Independence Boulevard
Salt Lake City, UT 84116

DAILY REPORT

Date 4/20/--

Order Number	Subtotal Amount	Tax Charged	Total Amount
	$	$	$
Total	$	$	$

Application 2-12
Calculate Percentages

OBJECTIVE

Upon completion of this application, you will be able to calculate percentages of income.

INSTRUCTIONS

1. Calculate the Total Income from all services.

2. Calculate the Percentage for each service by dividing Income from each service by the Total Income. (Example: $1,649.69 divided by the Total Income.) Remember to set the decimal selector mode at zero and then press the percent (%) key to get the result.

When you have completed Unit 2, ask your teacher the procedure for submitting this unit. Do not begin Unit 3 until your teacher has approved Unit 2.

Pronto Print Place

Daily Report for 9/10/--

Service	Income	Percentage
Printing (Impression)	$ 1,649.69	
Docutex (Photocopying)	976.40	
Bind	2,365.43	
Shrink Wrap	300.00	
Drill	211.90	
Staple	105.15	
Film (Negatives) 8.5" x 11"	134.75	
Film (Negatives) 8.5" x 14"	369.30	
Film (Negatives) 11" x 17"	572.50	
Plates (8.5" x 11" & 8.5" x 14")	280.00	
Plates (11" x 17")	39.00	
Fold	175.00	
Stuff	490.00	
Total	$	

Unit 2
Applications Evaluation

Last Name   First Name

Refer to completed Applications 2-1 through 2-12 to answer the following questions. The total point value of all the questions for each application as well as the point value of each individual question is indicated by the numbers in parentheses. Leave the Points Earned column blank. Your teacher will complete it.

Application 2-1

Points Earned

Prepare Sales Reports (6) (2 each)

of 6

What was the total amount in checks for the week? _____

What was the total amount in bank card sales for the week less the bank card credits? _____

What was the total amount in cash receipts for the week? _____

Application 2-2

Complete Fund Drive Report (10) (Value beside each)

of 10

What was the total amount of contributions for Departments 143, 327, 440, 643, and 964? (3) _____

What was the total amount of contributions for Departments 282, 539, 707, 895, and 1010? (3) _____

What was the total number of contributors for Departments 143, 327, 440, 643, and 964? (2) _____

What was the total number of contributors for Departments 282, 539, 707, 895, and 1010? (2) _____

Application 2-3

Transfer and Calculate Cash Receipts (6) (2 each)

of 6

What was the combined amount collected by the Paisleys and Plaids teams? _____

What was the combined amount collected by the Pin Stripes and Prints teams? _____

What would have been the amount collected if there had been no Polka Dots team? _____

Application 2-4

Make Sales Comparisons (10) (Value beside each)

What were last month's total sales?	(1) _____
What were this month's total sales?	(1) _____
Was the difference in the totals for the two months an increase or a decrease?	(2) _____
What item had the greatest increase?	(2) _____
Suits make up what percentage of this month's total sales?	(2) _____
What is the percentage of increase/decrease from last month?	(2) _____

_____
of 10

Application 2-5

Calculate Sales Slips (18) (Value beside each)

What were the total receipts from gasoline for all slips?	(3) _____
What were the total receipts from both regular and hand washes for all slips?	(4) _____
What were the total receipts from hand waxes for all slips?	(3) _____
What were the total receipts from the sale of all types of floor mats for all slips?	(3) _____
What were the total receipts from the sale of cup holders for all slips?	(3) _____
What were the total receipts (including sales tax) from Slips 111-120?	(2) _____

_____
of 18

Application 2-6

Prepare Earnings Report (12) (Value beside each)

How many books were sold for both stores combined?	(1) _____
What was the Total Sales amount for both stores combined?	(1) _____
What was the combined Sales amount of Biography, Classics, and Drama books for both stores?	(2) _____
What was the combined Sales amount of Action/Adventure, Fantasy, Mystery, and Science Fiction books for both stores?	(2) _____
What was the combined Sales amount of Cooking, Gardening, Home Care, and Hobbies/Crafts books for both stores?	(2) _____
What was the combined Sales amount of Fitness/Nutrition, Medical Care, Sports, and Self-Help books for both stores?	(2) _____
What was the combined Sales amount of Travel, Languages, Entertainment, and Local Interest books for both stores?	(2) _____

_____
of 12

Application 2-7

Update Inventory Reports (12) (3 each)

What was the combined inventory of Pop cassettes and CDs?

of 12

What was the combined inventory of R&B and Jazz CDs and DVDs?

What was the combined inventory of Country and Gospel VHSs?

What was the combined inventory available for sale 6/15 of Apparel, Novelties, and Posters?

Application 2-8

Determine Average Sales (12) (3 each)

What were the total sales for the Oceanview, Tides Town, and Pacific Grove branches?

of 12

What were the total sales for the Alabama, Georgia, Louisiana, and North Carolina branches?

What was the total number of sales staff in branches with sales of $7,000 or greater?

What was the sum of Average Staff Sales for the Missoula, Albuquerque, and Rapid City branches?

Application 2-9

Compute Profit (19) (Value beside each)

What was the total number of pairs of shoes sold? (2)_____

of 19

What was the combined sales income for the two highest-selling shoe types? (4)_____

What was the combined sales income for the two lowest-selling shoe types? (4)_____

What was the combined profit from the sale of crosstrainer, fitness, and running shoes? (4)_____

Golf shoes accounted for what percentage of the net profit? (5)_____

Application 2-10

Complete Guest Checks and Prepare Report (13) (Value beside each)

What was the total number of persons served? (1)_____

of 13

What was the total amount received for food (not including tax)? (1)_____

What percent of the total amount received (food plus tax) was food? (3)_____

If all persons on Check #102817 paid the same amount, what was the cost of each person's meal (including tax)? (3)_____

What was the average check amount? (2)_____

If server No. 18 received a 15% tip on the total amount collected from all checks, how much did the server receive in tips for the day? (3)_____

Application 2-11

Prepare Order Forms (26) (2 each)

What were the total sales from all orders, excluding sales tax? _____

What were the total sales (including sales tax) from Orders 127-131? _____

What were the total sales (including sales tax) from Orders 132-136? _____

What were the total charges for all types of special paper orders? _____

What was the total number of sheets printed in black, one side? _____

What was the total number of sheets printed in black, two sides? _____

What was the total number of sheets printed in two colors, one side? _____

What was the total number of sheets printed in two colors, two sides? _____

What was the total number of sheets printed in three colors, one side? _____

What was the total number of sheets printed in three colors, two sides? _____

Do not include sales tax or special paper amounts in the following answers:

What was the total collected from all orders printed in black, one side? _____

What was the total collected from all orders printed in black, two sides? _____

What was the total collected from all orders printed in two colors, one side? _____

Application 2-12

Calculate Percentages (6) (2 each)

_____

of 6

What was the total income from all film negatives? _____

How many services provided 5% or less of the total income? _____

How many services provided 15% or more of the total income? _____

Grading Scale

A = 150–139 points
B = 138–128 points
C = 127–117 points
D = 116–106 points

Total Points Earned of 150 _____

Unit 2 Applications Evaluation Grade _____

Various Reports, Installment Buying, and Inventory

Name _____

Date Started _____

Date Completed _____

Unit 3 has 8 applications. Read the instructions carefully; do not seek help from your teacher until you have studied the instructions thoroughly. Unit 3 requires approximately 250 minutes. Estimate how much time to spend on each application and time your work to meet a deadline of 250 minutes. *Do not waste time.*

For each application, keep an accurate record of when you start and when you finish. Continue to verify your calculations.

When you have completed all 8 applications, ask your teacher the procedure for submitting this unit for approval. Do not begin Unit 4 until your teacher has approved Unit 3.

 **Unit Three Time Record**

Application	Time Stopped	Time Started	Minutes Required
3-1			
3-2			
3-3			
3-4			
3-5			
3-6			
3-7			
3-8			
Total Minutes Required			

_____
Teacher's Approval

Application 3-1
Complete Enrollment Reports

OBJECTIVES

Upon completion of this application, you will be able to:

1. Determine the percent change in freshman enrollment by major from year to year.

2. Determine each major's percent of the total college enrollment from year to year.

3. Determine the average enrollment for each year and by major for a three-year period.

INSTRUCTIONS

Complete the two enrollment reports as follows:

Part 1

1. For each major, calculate the percent change in enrollment between 2002 and 2003 by subtracting the smaller enrollment from the larger enrollment. Divide the result by the 2002 enrollment figure. Write the percentage in the Percent Change from 2002 column. Round to a whole number. If the percent change is a decrease, include a minus sign. (The first percent change has been completed for you.)

2. Following the same procedure, calculate the Percent Change from 2003 (change in enrollment between 2003 and 2004), and the Percent Change from 2004 (change in enrollment between 2004 and 2005).

3. Add each of the four enrollment columns. Round to whole numbers. Write the results in the Total row.

4. Using the enrollment column totals, calculate the percent change in total freshman enrollment for 2002, 2003, and 2004 by following the same procedures as in Step 1. Write the results in the Total row.

5. For each major, calculate the Average Enrollment by adding the enrollment for the years 2003, 2004, and 2005 and dividing by 3. Round to a whole number. Write the result in the Average Enrollment column.

6. Total the Average Enrollment column and calculate the average by dividing the Total by the number of majors. Crosscheck to verify that this average matches the result written in the Average Enrollment column.

Part 2

1. Transfer the four enrollment column totals to the Total row of the Part 2 table.

2. For each major and each year, calculate the Percent of Total Enrollment by dividing the total enrollment for the year by the number enrolled in the major for that year. You may input the first figure and press the division key, then input the second figure and press the percent key to obtain an automatic percentage. (The first percent of total enrollment has been completed for you.)

3. To calculate the Average enrollment for each year, divide the Total enrollment by the number of majors offered. Round to a whole number. Write the result in the Average row.

Part 1

PERCENT CHANGE IN FRESHMAN ENROLLMENT BY MAJOR 2002–2005								
MAJOR	2002 Enrollment	2003 Enrollment	Percent Change from 2002	2004 Enrollment	Percent Change from 2003	2005 Enrollment	Percent Change from 2004	Average Enrollment (last 3 years)
Business	1,357	1,248	-8	809		1,099		
Education	634	757		1,290		854		
Engineering	941	823		627		587		
Liberal Arts	952	1,039		894		613		
Nursing	1,054	1,319		1,396		1,231		
Pharmacy	1,158	1,284		1,200		1,398		
Social Science	638	559		897		467		
Total								

Part 2

PERCENT OF TOTAL FRESHMAN ENROLLMENT BY MAJOR 2002–2005								
MAJOR	2002 Enrollment	Percent of 2002 Total Enrollment	2003 Enrollment	Percent of 2003 Total Enrollment	2004 Enrollment	Percent of 2004 Total Enrollment	2005 Enrollment	Percent of 2005 Total Enrollment
Business	1,357	20	1,248		809		1,099	
Education	634		757		1,290		854	
Engineering	941		823		627		587	
Liberal Arts	952		1,039		894		613	
Nursing	1,054		1,319		1,396		1,231	
Pharmacy	1,158		1,284		1,200		1,398	
Social Science	638		559		897		467	
Total								
Average								

Application 3-2
Determine Installment Buying Costs

OBJECTIVES

Upon completion of this application, you will be able to:

1. Calculate the cost of installment buying.
2. Calculate the percent of add-on interest.

INSTRUCTIONS

To complete the Record of Installment Buying, follow these steps for each item purchased (the first item has been completed for you as an example):

1. Multiply the Monthly Payment (Column 1) by the Number of Payments (Column 2), then add the Down Payment (Column 3). Record the result in Column 4 (Installment Price).

2. Subtract the Original Cash Price (Column 5) from the Installment Price (Column 4). The difference is the Cost of Borrowing (interest). Record the interest in Column 6.

3. To calculate the Total Loan Percentage (Column 7), divide the Cost of Borrowing (Column 6) by the Original Cash Price (Column 5). Round the percentage to two decimal places and record the result in Column 7.

Record of Installment Buying

1 Monthly Payment	2 Number of Payments	3 Down Payment	4 Installment Price	5 Original Cash Price	6 Cost of Borrowing	7 Total Loan Percentage
$103.50	24	$100	$ 2,584.00	$2,000	$ 584.00	29.20
150.48	12	150		1,875		
175.26	36	175		6,000		
237.40	48	200		10,000		
375.60	24	225		8,300		
418.32	24	250		8,449		
541.67	36	300		15,800		
723.89	48	400		30,250		
918.27	60	500		45,200		
1,100.00	60	550		51,300		

Application 3-3

Prepare Departmental Expense Report

OBJECTIVES

Upon completion of this application, you will be able to:

1. Calculate reimbursable mileage.

2. Determine total expenses for a week for individual sales staff members.

3. Transfer data and complete a weekly departmental expense report.

INSTRUCTIONS

Complete each salesperson's expense report as follows (the first one has been completed for you as an example):

1. For each day, calculate reimbursable mileage by multiplying the number of miles traveled (shown in Car Miles Column 1) by $.325. Record the result in Car Miles Column 2. Round answers to two decimal places.

2. For each day, add across all the expenses and record the total.

3. Add down each column and record the total.

4. Verify the grand total for each salesperson by adding the Total column down and then by adding the bottom row of Totals across. The two figures should match.

Complete the Sales Department Expense Report as follows:

1. For each salesperson's expense report, add the Car Miles, Air Fare, Parking, Tolls, and Taxis totals for a combined Transportation total to be transferred to the report. Add the Meals and Lodging totals for a combined total to be transferred to the report. Add the Gratuities and Other totals for a combined total to be transferred to the report. These totals should match the totals on the expense reports.

2. Add across and down to calculate the totals on the report.

3. Verify the grand total for the week by adding the Total column down and the bottom row of Totals across. The two figures should match.

CLASSIC COMPUTERS

Name: Allen, Alvin

Week Ending: May 5

Department: Sales

Date	Transportation						Meals	Lodging	Gratuities	Other	Total
May	Car Miles 1	2	Air Fare	Parking	Tolls	Taxis					
1	213	$69.23	$	$ 1.25	$ .50	$	$25.70	$56.18	$	$	$ 152.86
2	156	50.70					31.75	70.11			$ 152.56
3	15	4.88		.50			37.62	70.11			$ 113.11
4	148	48.10			.50		21.60				$ 70.20
5											$
Totals		$172.91	$ —	$ 1.75	$1.00	$ —	$116.67	$196.40	$ —	$ —	$ 488.73

CLASSIC COMPUTERS

Name Boyle, Burt

Department Sales

Week Ending May 5

Date May	Car Miles 1	Car Miles 2	Transportation Air Fare	Parking	Tolls	Taxis	Meals	Lodging	Gratuities	Other	Total
1	10	$	$482.00	$ 10.00	$	$ 38.00	$ 27.54	$ 127.88	$ 5.00	$ 150.00	$
2				15.00		8.00	68.45	127.88	7.00		$
3				15.00		14.00	71.32	127.88	8.00		$
4				15.00		13.00	62.10	127.88	5.00		$
5	10			10.00		38.00	7.90		5.00		
Totals		$	482.00	$	$	$	$	$	$	$	$

CLASSIC COMPUTERS

Name Cook, Calvin

Department Sales

Week Ending May 5

Date May	Car Miles 1	Car Miles 2	Transportation Air Fare	Parking	Tolls	Taxis	Meals	Lodging	Gratuities	Other	Total
1	312	$	$	$	$ 1.50	$	$ 49.61	$ 63.03	$	$	$
2	56						55.82	68.05			$
3	48			.75			39.41	56.81			$
4	127				1.50		49.01	64.81			$
5	139				.50		20.16				$
Totals		$	$	$	$	$	$	$	$	$	$

CLASSIC COMPUTERS

Name Davis, David

Department Sales

Week Ending May 5

Date May	Car Miles 1 2	Transportation Air Fare	Parking	Tolls	Taxis	Meals	Lodging	Gratuities	Other	Total
1	102	$	$ .75	$ 1.00	$	$ 45.25	$ 77.25	$	$	$
2	95		1.25			55.35	67.75			
3	89		8.00			39.25	72.27			
4	98		4.00			64.19	69.73			
5	132			1.00		10.28				
Totals		$	$	$	$	$	$	$	$	$

CLASSIC COMPUTERS

Name Ellis, Edwin

Department Sales

Week Ending May 5

Date May	Car Miles 1 2	Transportation Air Fare	Parking	Tolls	Taxis	Meals	Lodging	Gratuities	Other	Total
1	6	$ 515.00	$ 10.00	$	$ 40.00	$ 29.46	$ 137.45	$ 10.00	$	$
2			15.00			58.32	137.45	6.00	5.75	
3	6	515.00	10.00			10.25		6.00		
4										
5										
Totals		$	$	$	$	$	$	$	$	$

CLASSIC COMPUTERS

Name Fuller, Frank **Week Ending** May 5

Department Sales

Date May	Car Miles 1	Car Miles 2	Transportation Air Fare	Parking	Tolls	Taxis	Meals	Lodging	Gratuities	Other	Total
1	251		$	$ 6.00	$	$	$ 15.20	$ 55.68	$	$	$
2	251						9.10				
3	8		345.00	10.00		13.00	25.19	74.19	5.00		
4				15.00			56.78	74.19	11.00		
5	8		345.00	10.00		13.00	18.65		8.00		
Totals			$	$	$	$	$	$	$	$	$

CLASSIC COMPUTERS

Name Garrison, Greg **Week Ending** May 5

Department Sales

Date May	Car Miles 1	Car Miles 2	Transportation Air Fare	Parking	Tolls	Taxis	Meals	Lodging	Gratuities	Other	Total
1	318		$	$	$ 1.50	$	$ 25.19	$ 55.35	$	$	$
2	137			2.50			36.08	56.75			
3	98				2.00		32.40	59.75			
4	65			3.00			31.79	58.42			
5	214						12.35				
Totals			$	$	$	$	$	$	$	$	$

CLASSIC COMPUTERS

Name Jensen, Jennifer Week Ending _____ May 5

Department Sales

Date May	Car Miles 1	2	Transportation Air Fare	Parking	Tolls	Taxis	Meals	Lodging	Gratuities	Other	Total
1	26	$	$ 568.00	$ 10.00	$	$ 22.00	$ 30.25	$ 128.97	$ 3.00	$	$
2				15.00		18.00	39.86	128.97	5.00	10.00	$
3	26		568.00	5.00		22.00	10.46		3.00		$
4	75						43.21	87.64			$
5	75						17.90				$
Totals		$	$	$	$	$	$	$	$	$	$

CLASSIC COMPUTERS

Name Mann, Mark Week Ending _____ May 5

Department Sales

Date May	Car Miles 1	2	Transportation Air Fare	Parking	Tolls	Taxis	Meals	Lodging	Gratuities	Other	Total
1	106	$	$	$ .75	$ 1.50	$	$ 35.35	$ 86.50	$	$	$
2	124			.50	1.50		39.85	79.44		8.00	$
3	118			.25	1.00		31.60	82.21			$
4	105			1.25	.50		33.15	76.98			$
5	167			.30	1.00		5.98				$
Totals		$	$	$	$	$	$	$	$	$	$

CLASSIC COMPUTERS

Name   Parks, Paige

Department   Sales

Week Ending   May 5

Date May	Car Miles 1	2	Transportation Air Fare	Parking	Tolls	Taxis	Meals	Lodging	Gratuities	Other	Total
1	67	$	$	$	$ 1.00	$	$ 19.87	$ 64.90	$	$	$
2	248			2.00			34.54	66.70			
3	184				1.50		27.68	62.18			
4	105			1.50			32.15	63.55			
5	111						8.83				
Totals		$	$	$	$	$	$	$	$	$	$

CLASSIC COMPUTERS

Name   Richards, Rick

Department   Sales

Week Ending   May 5

Date May	Car Miles 1	2	Transportation Air Fare	Parking	Tolls	Taxis	Meals	Lodging	Gratuities	Other	Total
1	32	$	$ 437.50	$ 15.00	$	$ 23.00	$ 57.65	$ 138.55	$ 10.00	$	$
2				15.00		21.00	65.40	138.55	9.00	12.00	
3				15.00		15.00	68.10	138.55	12.00		
4				15.00		6.00	55.90	138.55	13.00		
5	32			10.00		17.00	14.23		10.00		
Totals		$	$ 437.50	$	$	$	$	$	$	$	$

116

CLASSIC COMPUTERS

Name   Stevens, Stephen

Department   Sales   Week Ending _____ May 5

Date May	Car Miles 1	2 $	Transportation Air Fare $	Parking $	Tolls $	Taxis $	Meals $	Lodging $	Gratuities $	Other $	Total $
1	253						14.80	61.25			
2	210						16.83	59.87			
3	145						9.47				
4											
5	217						13.16				
Totals		$	$	$	$	$	$	$	$	$	$

CLASSIC COMPUTERS

Name   Thompson, Thomas

Department   Sales   Week Ending _____ May 5

Date May	Car Miles 1	2 $	Transportation Air Fare $	Parking $	Tolls $	Taxis $	Meals $	Lodging $	Gratuities $	Other $	Total $
1	13		198.00	10.00	.50	19.00	40.66	133.46	12.00		
2	13		198.00	10.00	.50	25.00	21.75		8.00		
3											
4											
5	256			3.00	1.50		13.46		2.00		
Totals		$	$	$	$	$	$	$	$	$	$

CLASSIC COMPUTERS

Name _West, Walter_ Week Ending _____ May 5 _____

Department _Sales_

Date May	Car Miles 1	2	Transportation Air Fare	Parking	Tolls	Taxis	Meals	Lodging	Gratuities	Other	Total
1	76	$	$	$ 2.00	$	$	$ 15.80	$ 79.12	$	$	$
2	89			3.00			16.83	78.32			$
3	142			2.50			19.72	80.45			$
4	201			1.00			18.97	77.97			$
5	115			.50			7.08				$
Totals		$	$	$	$	$	$	$	$	$	$

CLASSIC COMPUTERS

Name _Zandy, Zack_ Week Ending _____ May 5 _____

Department _Sales_

Date May	Car Miles 1	2	Transportation Air Fare	Parking	Tolls	Taxis	Meals	Lodging	Gratuities	Other	Total
1	132	$	$	$	$	$	$ 11.77	$	$	$	$
2	19		312.00	10.00		18.00	26.93	157.60	6.00	175.00	$
3				15.00		15.00	38.76	157.60			$
4				15.00		22.00	41.65	157.60	6.00		$
5	19			10.00		18.00	10.01				$
Totals		$	312.00	$	$	$	$	$	$	$	$

CLASSIC COMPUTERS
SALES DEPARTMENT EXPENSE REPORT
Week Ending ___May 5___

Name	Transportation	Meals/Lodging	Gratuities/Other	Total
Allen, Alvin	$	$	$	$
Boyle, Burt				
Cook, Calvin				
Davis, David				
Ellis, Edwin				
Fuller, Frank				
Garrison, Greg				
Jensen, Jennifer				
Mann, Mark				
Parks, Paige				
Richards, Rick				
Stevens, Stephen				
Thompson, Thomas				
West, Walter				
Zandy, Zack				
Totals	$	$	$	$

Application 3-4

Calculate Fuel Amount Pumped

OBJECTIVES

Upon completion of this application, you will be able to:

1. Calculate the number of gallons of gasoline sold by grade for a day.

2. Transfer data and complete a daily report of total customers served and total gallons pumped.

INSTRUCTIONS

Write the current date in the space provided at the top of Form A and Form B. Complete Form B by using the figures shown on Form A as follows (the first line of Form B has been completed for you):

1. For each grade of gasoline purchased (Regular, Plus, or Premium), count the number of customers served each hour. For each hour, write in the appropriate columns on Form B the number of customers served each grade of gasoline. From 7:00 to 8:00, eight customers purchased Regular; six customers purchased Plus; and three customers purchased Premium (Columns 1, 3, and 5 on Form B).

2. Because gasoline is measured in thousandths of a gallon, set your calculator for three decimal places. For each grade of gasoline, add the number of gallons pumped each hour. Write the totals in the appropriate columns on Form B. From 7:00 to 8:00, 80.274 gallons of Regular, 68.635 of Plus, and 48.892 of Premium gasoline were pumped (Columns 2, 4, and 6).

3. On Form B, calculate the total number of customers served each hour by adding the figures for each of the three grades of gasoline. Write the totals in Column 7 on Form B. The total of 17 customers was calculated by adding the figures in Columns 1, 3, and 5.

4. On Form B, calculate the total number of gallons pumped each hour by adding the figures for each of the three grades of gasoline. Write the totals in Column 8 on Form B. The total of 197.801 gallons was calculated by adding the figures in Columns 2, 4, and 6.

5. On Form B, add each of the eight columns; write the totals at the bottoms of the columns. Add the totals for Columns 1, 3, and 5 to verify the total for Column 7. Add the totals for Columns 2, 4, and 6 to verify the total for Column 8.

Form A

Westside Auto Service, Inc.

1390 Cleveland Avenue, West
Burlington, VT 05401-1335

Date _____

DAILY TOTAL GALLONS PUMPED

Time	Regular	Plus	Premium
7:00 8:00	5.678 18.903 5.662 11.237 16.987 10.870 4.586 6.351	18.777 3.439 12.675 10.050 7.842 15.852	20.964 17.428 10.500
8:00 9:00	17.945 12.408 21.111 5.000 20.375 12.835	10.776 6.588 17.014 16.233	18.111 2.932 5.123 5.664 11.386 8.443
9:00 10:00	6.666 3.987 11.574 18.555 20.347 2.789	16.000 12.000 1.332 1.787 4.987 9.017	19.564 6.998 5.543 22.112 21.842
10:00 11:00	10.376 6.345 12.345 1.500 8.879 20.357	9.666 15.546 16.636	22.696 20.297 6.658 14.579 7.887
11:00 12:00	15.678 8.903 14.662 13.237 12.987 9.870 4.586 16.371	8.717 13.349 22.675 11.950 17.834 15.258	21.964 7.458 9.500 8.070 18.759
12:00 1:00	8.547 23.349 20.675 21.950 17.483 25.258	10.367 6.435 21.345 15.000 18.879 23.547	28.161 22.392 25.213 5.646 19.386 18.443
1:00 2:00	5.878 8.903 14.673 23.437 14.767 1.870	8.779 19.495 25.672 17.957	21.646 27.459 8.507 18.674
2:00 3:00	10.076 16.588 27.014 18.233	19.236 25.546 16.487	20.645 11.998 14.237
3:00 4:00	13.021 9.589 4.567 9.345 11.987	16.212 8.843 8.876	9.256 11.234
4:00 5:00	20.201 16.920 8.234 11.579 3.579 6.686	10.534 4.743 4.945 4.654	12.593
5:00 6:00	3.011 8.133 13.022 12.843 11.424 19.679 9.335 18.366 25.795 14.432	5.612 16.521 6.345 12.754 13.867 7.155 6.378	11.789 20.198 21.787 11.865 9.154 6.843 12.532
6:00 7:00	26.897 11.780 5.486 16.351	8.717 5.436 14.679	18.342 4.786 16.553
	8.675 8.913 6.562 12.273	18.052 8.742 25.582	10.964 12.483 15.973
	.223 5.934	3.745 12.156 3.745	15.267 8.878 11.289 8.809
	8	5.587 5.554 9.276	15.943 9.154
		13.987 5.987	9.541

121

Form B

Westside Auto Service, Inc.

1390 Cleveland Avenue, West
Burlington, VT 05401-1335

Date _____

DAILY TOTAL GALLONS PUMPED

Time	Regular		Plus		Premium		Total	
	1 Customers Served	2 Gallons Pumped	3 Customers Served	4 Gallons Pumped	5 Customers Served	6 Gallons Pumped	7 Customers Served	8 Gallons Pumped
7:00 8:00	8	80.274	6	68.635	3	48.892	17	197.801
8:00 9:00								
9:00 10:00								
10:00 11:00								
11:00 12:00								
12:00 1:00								
1:00 2:00								
2:00 3:00								
3:00 4:00								
4:00 5:00								
5:00 6:00								
6:00 7:00								
7:00 8:00								
8:00 9:00								
9:00 10:00								
10:00 11:00								
Total								

Application 3-5

Prepare Car Rental Contracts

OBJECTIVES

Upon completion of this application, you will be able to:

1. Prepare an auto rental contract.
2. Determine auto rental charges.
3. Prepare a daily business report.

INSTRUCTIONS

The contracts are arranged according to the Date the vehicle was rented and Time Out. Follow these steps to determine how the first contract was completed:

1. On the contract for Chang Choi, locate the Type Rental (Standard). Locate the Type Vehicle (Full Size). Refer to the Standard Rental Rate Chart and locate Full Size under Type of Vehicle. Read across the Full Size line to determine the rates per Hour, Day, Week, Month, and Mile, and the one-way drop-off charge. The weekly and mile figures are written on the contract next to Rate. (194.95 and .32 are written on the first contract and the $30 Drop Charge is circled.) If a renter returns a car to a city other than where it was rented, the $30 Drop Charge is circled and added to the basic rental charge.

2. In the Odometer Reading section of the contract, subtract the Leaving figure (172) from the Returning figure (852); the difference (680) is written on the Miles Driven line.

3. At the bottom of the contract, 680 Miles @ .32 is written. (You calculated the 680 miles when you subtracted, and the Rental Rate Chart shows .32 as the per mile rate.) Multiply 680 by .32 to obtain 217.60. This amount is written on the Miles line in the Charges column.

4. In the Charges column, 224.95 is written on the first line because Week is circled on the contract next to Rate, and 194.95 is shown on the Rental Rate Chart as the Week rate.

5. Hourly Charges apply to contracts when renters keep the vehicles longer than the agreed time. (For example, if someone rented a vehicle for one day on Monday at 7:35 a.m. and returned it on Tuesday at 10:30 a.m., the Day rate stopped at 7:35 a.m. on Tuesday. In addition to the Day rate, the renter would be charged for three hours at the Hour rate. Use the closest number of hours; 2 hours 55 minutes would be a charge of three hours.) To determine the number of hours to charge for overtime, refer to the top of the contract. Chang Choi rented the vehicle at 7:00 a.m. on Wednesday, 3/11, for one week. He returned the vehicle at 9:00 a.m. on Wednesday, 3/18. He kept the vehicle for one week but was two hours late returning it. Charge him for the two hours. In the middle of the contract next to Rate, 13.21 is shown as the Hour rate. Multiply 13.21 by 2 to obtain 26.42. This amount is written in the Charges column on the line for Hourly Charges. If a vehicle is returned more than three hours late, there is no hourly charge; instead, the renter is charged for one extra day.

6. Insurance rates are circled. These rates are per day. Multiply the rate by the number of days the vehicle was rented (8.95 x 7 = 62.65). On the Insurance line in the Charges column, 62.65 is written. If None is written on the Insurance line of the contract, the renter did not purchase coverage. If both 8.95 and 1.95 are circled, add the two figures and then multiply by the number of days of coverage.

7. In the Odometer Reading section of the contract next to Gas Tank Reading, you will find a fraction or the words Full or Empty. If a renter fills the gas tank before returning the vehicle, no additional gasoline charges are incurred. If a fraction or Empty is recorded next to Gas Tank Reading, the renter must be charged for the tank to be filled. Refer to the Additional

Gasoline Charges chart. Locate the Type of Vehicle (Full Size). The fraction 7/8 is written on the Chang Choi contract; read across the Full Size line to determine the additional charge (9.10). This amount is written on the Gasoline Charges line in the Charges column.

8. Subtotal the charges by adding the figures in the Charges column; the subtotal is written on the Subtotal line (540.72). Multiply the Subtotal figure by 8 1/2% (.085) to calculate the sales tax, which is written on the Sales Tax line (45.96).

9. Add the Subtotal figure and the Sales Tax figure to calculate the total charges, which is written on the Total Charges line (586.68).

10. Complete the remaining contracts by following the procedures given in Steps 1-9.

After you have completed all the contracts, complete the Daily Business Report as follows:

1. Locate at the top of each contract above Time In the time each vehicle was returned.

   a. List the contracts on the report in the order in which the vehicles were returned. The first vehicle returned in the morning will be listed first, and the last vehicle returned before midnight will be listed last.

   b. List each vehicle on a separate line. Read across the columns of the report and transfer the information needed from each contract to the report.

2. Total the columns on the report. Add across each column total to verify that the Total Charges column total is correct.

TEMPO AUTO RENTAL, INC.
GOVERNMENT RENTAL RATE CHART

Type of Vehicle	Hour*	Day	Week	Month	Mile
Economy	10.56	31.00	134.55	534.00	.15
Compact	11.00	33.00	154.95	600.00	.15
Intermediate	11.56	35.00	194.55	730.20	.25
Full Size	12.00	36.00	204.95	771.80	.25
Luxury	13.67	39.00	275.80	827.40	.30
SUV	14.95	46.00	290.55	871.65	.35
Van	16.61	58.00	380.00	1,140.00	.35

CORPORATE RENTAL RATE CHART

Type of Vehicle	Hour*	Day	Week	Month	Mile
Economy	12.50	35.00	175.00	652.00	.17
Compact	13.22	39.00	180.00	720.00	.17
Intermediate	13.87	42.00	186.00	744.00	.28
Full Size	14.60	45.00	190.00	760.00	.28
Luxury	15.90	48.00	195.00	780.00	.315
SUV	16.95	52.00	201.00	804.00	.37
Van	18.00	55.00	280.00	1,100.00	.37

STANDARD RENTAL RATE CHART

Type of Vehicle	Hour*	Day	Week	Month	Mile
Economy	11.50	33.95	175.95	655.80	.21
Compact	12.00	39.95	179.95	699.95	.21
Intermediate	12.60	42.00	189.95	759.95	.32
Full Size	13.21	56.70	194.95	839.95	.32
Luxury	18.99	84.95	460.00	888.00	.335
SUV	19.50	87.55	458.50	995.95	.335
Van	18.99	89.95	477.95	1,280.00	.38

Insurance, Per Day Rate:	Personal Effects Protection	$1.95	Loss Damage Waiver	$20.99
	Liability	$8.95	Personal Accident	$ 3.00

A driver's license and one major credit card is required to rent a vehicle.
Minimum age to rent a vehicle is 25. Proof of age is required.
*Hourly rate applies to the use of a vehicle for up to 3 hours beyond the daily, weekly, or monthly rate. If the vehicle is returned more than 3 hours late, the renter is charged an additional day.

TEMPO AUTO RENTAL, INC.
ADDITIONAL GASOLINE CHARGES

Type of Vehicle	7/8 Tank	3/4 Tank	5/8 Tank	1/2 Tank	3/8 Tank	1/4 Tank	1/8 Tank	Empty Tank
Economy	7.28	14.56	26.84	29.12	36.40	43.68	50.96	58.24
Compact	7.28	14.56	26.84	29.12	36.40	43.68	50.96	58.24
Intermediate	9.10	18.20	27.30	36.40	45.50	54.60	63.70	72.80
Full Size	9.10	18.20	27.30	36.40	45.50	54.60	63.70	72.80
Luxury	10.01	20.02	30.03	40.04	50.05	60.06	70.07	80.08
SUV	11.38	22.75	34.13	45.50	56.87	68.25	79.65	91.00
Van	11.38	22.75	34.13	45.50	56.87	68.25	79.65	91.00

Form 1 (Contract No. 8021)

Tempo Auto Rental, Inc.
ALBUQUERQUE, NM 87105-2497

7:00 a.m. Wednesday 3/11/--
Time Out Day Date

9:00 a.m. Wednesday 3/18/--
Time In Day Date

One-way drop phoenix, AZ

Name Chang Choi

Address 2635 West Aberdeen Drive San Jose, CA 95130-2866

Representing Self (artist)

Type Payment Credit Card   **Type Vehicle** Full Size

Drop Chg (30) *(circled)*

Type Rental
- Government ___
- Corporate ___
- Standard ✓

Rate: ___ Hour 194.95 Day / (Week) ___ Month .32 Mile

Odometer Reading:
- Returning 852   Vehicle No. 660
- Leaving 172   Gas Tank Reading 7/8
- Miles Driven 680

	CHARGES
Basic Rental	224.95
680 Miles @ .32	217.60
Hourly Charges (If applicable)	26.42
Insurance: (\$8.95) \$1.95 \$20.99 \$3.00	
PER DAY for 7 day(s)	62.65
Gasoline Charges	9.10
Subtotal	540.72
Sales Tax	45.96
Total Charges	586.68

CONTRACT NO. 8021

Form 2 (Contract No. 8122)

Tempo Auto Rental, Inc.
ALBUQUERQUE, NM 87105-2497

7:40 a.m. Wednesday 3/11/--
Time Out Day Date

8:40 a.m. Wednesday 3/18/--
Time In Day Date

Name Sandra Sue Semmes

Address 8275 Lincoln Lane North Miami Beach, FL 33139-7369

Representing City of Miami Beach

Type Payment Credit Card   **Type Vehicle** Intermediate

Drop Chg 30

Type Rental
- Government ___
- Corporate ___
- Standard ___ ✓

Rate: ___ Hour ___ Day / (Week) ___ Month ___ Mile

Odometer Reading:
- Returning 539   Vehicle No. 462
- Leaving 168   Gas Tank Reading Empty
- Miles Driven

	CHARGES
Basic Rental	
___ Miles @	
Hourly Charges (If applicable)	
Insurance: (\$8.95) \$1.95 \$20.99 \$3.00	
PER DAY for 7 day(s)	
Gasoline Charges	
Subtotal	
Sales Tax	
Total Charges	

CONTRACT NO. 8122

Form 8128

Tempo Auto Rental, Inc.
ALBUQUERQUE, NM 87105-2497

7:35 a.m. _Sunday_ 3/15/--
Time Out   Day   Date

9:30 a.m. _Wednesday_ 3/18/--
Time In   Day   Date

Name _Reginald Rix, Esq._

Address _2973 Robertsdale Road   Lansing, MI 48910-1869_

Representing _Self (attorney)_

Type Payment _Personal Check_   Type Vehicle _Luxury_   30 Drop Chg

Type Rental
Government ___
Corporate ___
Standard ✓

Rate: ___ Hour 3 (Day) Week Month Mile

Odometer Reading: Vehicle No. _759_

Returning _503_   Gas Tank Reading _5/8_
Leaving _097_
Miles Driven ___

CHARGES

Basic Rental ___

Miles @ ___

Hourly Charges (If applicable)
Insurance: $8.95 $1.95 ($20.99) $3.00
PER DAY for ___ day(s)

Gasoline Charges ___

Subtotal ___
Sales Tax ___
Total Charges ___

CONTRACT NO. **8128**

Form 8159

Tempo Auto Rental, Inc.
ALBUQUERQUE, NM 87105-2497

7:45 a.m. _Saturday_ 3/14/--
Time Out   Day   Date

9:40 a.m. _Wednesday_ 3/18/--
Time In   Day   Date

Name _William W. Williamson_

Address _9136 Atlantic Cove   Wilmington, DE 19711-6233_

Representing _State Department of Revenue_

Type Payment _Credit Card_   Type Vehicle _Compact_   30 Drop Chg

Type Rental
Government ✓
Corporate ___
Standard ___

Rate: ___ Hour 4 (Day) Week Month Mile

Odometer Reading: Vehicle No. _533_

Returning _406_   Gas Tank Reading _Full_
Leaving _128_
Miles Driven ___

CHARGES

Basic Rental ___

Miles @ ___

Hourly Charges (If applicable)
Insurance: ($8.95) $1.95 $20.99 $3.00
PER DAY for _4_ day(s)

Gasoline Charges ___

Subtotal ___
Sales Tax ___
Total Charges ___

CONTRACT NO. **8159**

129

Tempo Auto Rental, Inc.
ALBUQUERQUE, NM 87105-2497

7:55 a.m.	Sunday	3/15/--
Time Out	Day	Date
7:45 a.m.	Wednesday	3/18/--
Time In	Day	Date

Name Kelly X. Keele
Address 276 Cedar Hill Drive, Apt. 1193 St. Louis, MO 63128-2114
Representing Midwestern University

Type Payment Cash   **Type Vehicle** Economy   30 **Drop Chg**

Type Rental
Government ✓
Corporate ___
Standard ___

Rate: ___ Hour 3 (Day) ___ Week ___ Month ___ Mile

Odometer Reading: Vehicle No. 996
Returning 992   Gas Tank Reading 3/8
Leaving 539
Miles Driven ___

CHARGES
Basic Rental ___
___ Miles @ ___
Hourly Charges (If applicable)
Insurance: $8.95 $1.95 $20.99 $3.00
PER DAY for ___ day(s) ___
Gasoline Charges ___
Subtotal ___
Sales Tax ___

CONTRACT NO. 8129   Total Charges ___

Tempo Auto Rental, Inc.
ALBUQUERQUE, NM 87105-2497

7:35 a.m.	Monday	3/16/--
Time Out	Day	Date
6:30 a.m.	Wednesday	3/18/--
Time In	Day	Date

Name Josephine J. Joseph
Address 2964 Osborne Place Rye, NY 10580-1342
Representing Chase National Bank

Type Payment Credit Card   **Type Vehicle** Luxury   30 **Drop Chg**

Type Rental
Government ___
Corporate ___
Standard ✓

Rate: ___ Hour 2 (Day) ___ Week ___ Month ___ Mile

Odometer Reading: Vehicle No. 722
Returning 394   Gas Tank Reading 1/4
Leaving 206
Miles Driven ___

CHARGES
Basic Rental ___
___ Miles @ ___
Hourly Charges (If applicable)
Insurance: ($8.95) $1.95 $20.99 $3.00
PER DAY for 2 day(s) ___
Gasoline Charges ___
Subtotal ___
Sales Tax ___

CONTRACT NO. 8140   Total Charges ___

Tempo Auto Rental, Inc.
ALBUQUERQUE, NM 87105-2497

7:05 a.m. Wednesday 3/18/--
Time Out — Day — Date

10:45 p.m. Wednesday 3/18/--
Time In — Day — Date

Name
Jerry J. Truman

Address
2973 Forest Hills Drive Southern Pines, NC 28387-4628

Representing
Old Southern Furniture Mart

Type Payment _Company Check_   Type Vehicle _SUV_   30 — Drop Chg

Type Rental
Government ____
Corporate ✓   Rate: ____ / ____ / ____ / ____ / ____
Standard ____   Hour / (Day) / Week / Month / Mile

Odometer Reading: Vehicle No. _821_

Returning _5262_   Gas Tank Reading _1/2_

Leaving _5021_

Miles Driven ____

CHARGES

Basic Rental ____

Miles @ ____

Hourly Charges (If applicable)
Insurance: ($8.95) ($1.95) $20.99 $3.00 ____
PER DAY for _1_ day(s) ____

Gasoline Charges ____

Subtotal ____

Sales Tax ____

CONTRACT NO. 8167   Total Charges ____

Tempo Auto Rental, Inc.
ALBUQUERQUE, NM 87105-2497

7:15 a.m. Wednesday 3/18/--
Time Out — Day — Date

8:30 p.m. Wednesday 3/18/--
Time In — Day — Date

Name
Ginger Hennessy

Address
2973 Courtney Terrace Denton, TX 76201-2296

Representing
Hubble, Inc.

Type Payment _Company Check_   Type Vehicle _Intermediate_   30 — Drop Chg

Type Rental
Government ____
Corporate ✓   Rate: ____ / ____ / ____ / ____ / ____
Standard ____   Hour / (Day) / Week / Month / Mile

Odometer Reading: Vehicle No. _318_

Returning _652_   Gas Tank Reading _1/4_

Leaving _411_

Miles Driven ____

CHARGES

Basic Rental ____

Miles @ ____

Hourly Charges (If applicable)
Insurance: ($8.95) $1.95 $20.99 ($3.00) ____
PER DAY for _1_ day(s) ____

Gasoline Charges ____

Subtotal ____

Sales Tax ____

CONTRACT NO. 8168   Total Charges ____

131

Form 1 (top)

Tempo Auto Rental, Inc.
ALBUQUERQUE, NM 87105-2497

7:30 a.m. Wednesday 3/18/--
Time Out — Day — Date

3:05 p.m. Wednesday 3/18/--
Time In — Day — Date

One-Way drop Cannon A.F.B, Clovis NM

Name Joel Jefferson, Major U.S.A.F

Address 629 S.W. 156th Street Homestead, FL 33039-7066

Representing Homestead A.F.B

Type Payment Traveler's Check   Type Vehicle Van

Type Rental
Government
Corporate ✓
Standard

Rate: —— Hour / (Day) Week Month Mile

Odometer Reading:
Vehicle No. 328
Returning 883   Gas Tank Reading 3/4
Leaving 628
Miles Driven ——

CHARGES
Basic Rental ——
—— Miles @ ——
Hourly Charges (If applicable) ——
Insurance: ($8.95) $1.95 $20.99 $3.00
PER DAY for 1 day(s)
Gasoline Charges ——
Subtotal ——
Sales Tax ——

CONTRACT NO. **8170**   Total Charges ——

Drop Chg (30)

Form 2 (bottom)

Tempo Auto Rental, Inc.
ALBUQUERQUE, NM 87105-2497

7:25 a.m. Wednesday 3/18/--
Time Out — Day — Date

9:50 p.m. Wednesday 3/18/--
Time In — Day — Date

Name Bernice Bukaty

Address 6957 Laket Avenue, Apt. 206 Madison, WI 53710-3115

Representing Central Hospital

Type Payment Credit Card   Type Vehicle Full Size

Type Rental
Government
Corporate ✓
Standard

Rate: —— Hour / (Day) Week Month Mile

Odometer Reading:
Vehicle No. 107
Returning 792   Gas Tank Reading 1/8
Leaving 499
Miles Driven ——

CHARGES
Basic Rental ——
—— Miles @ ——
Hourly Charges (If applicable) ——
Insurance: ($8.95) $1.95 $20.99 $3.00
PER DAY for 1 day(s)
Gasoline Charges ——
Subtotal ——
Sales Tax ——

CONTRACT NO. **8169**   Total Charges ——

Drop Chg (30)

132

Tempo

Auto Rental, Inc.
Albuquerque, NM 87105-2497
DAILY BUSINESS REPORT
Date ___3/18/___--___

Contract Number	Renter's Name (Last, Initials)	Vehicle Number	Basic Rental	Mileage Charges	Hourly Charges	Insurance Charges	Gasoline Charges	Sales Tax	Total Charges
			$	$	$	$	$	$	$
		Total	$	$	$	$	$	$	$

Application 3-6
Complete Linen Inventory

OBJECTIVE

Upon completion of this application, you will be able to calculate a net inventory.

INSTRUCTIONS

Complete the Linen Inventory form by following these steps:

1. For any item for which a current purchase has been made, add across the figures in Column 2 (Begin on Hand) and Column 3 (Current Purchases); write the total in Column 4 (To Account For). For items for which no current purchases have been made, transfer the figure from Column 2 to Column 4.

2. To calculate the Loss for each item, subtract the figure in Column 5 (Transfer to Salvage) from the figure in Column 4 (To Account For). From the result, subtract the figure in Column 6 (End on Hand). Write the final result in Column 7 (Loss).

3. Add each column; write the total at the bottom of each column. Add the totals for Columns 2 and 3 to verify the total for Column 4. Subtract the total of Column 5 from the total of Column 4, then subtract the total of Column 6 to verify the total of Column 7.

LINEN INVENTORY

Southern Hospitality Hotel **Date** *November 19, 20--*

1	2	3	4	5	6	7
Description	Begin on Hand	Current Purchases	To Account For	Transfer to Salvage	End on Hand	Loss
Blankets, Twin	37	0		9	24	
Blankets, Standard	600	125		15	703	
Blankets, Queen	225	0		17	199	
Blankets, King	188	50		21	198	
Sheets, Twin	225	0		32	182	
Sheets, Standard	1,800	432		382	1,827	
Sheets, Queen	675	0		110	562	
Sheets, King	563	0		64	487	
Bed Pads, Twin	100	15		2	100	
Bed Pads, Standard	800	0		65	726	
Bed Pads, Queen	300	75		13	354	
Bed Pads, King	250	0		0	250	
Pillows	2,500	255		57	2,671	
Face Cloths	3,700	864		286	3,424	
Hand Towels	2,850	288		198	2,352	
Bath Towels	4,750	576		247	4,318	
Bath Mats	1,325	144		39	1,358	
Totals						

Application 3-7
Calculate China Inventory

OBJECTIVES

Upon completion of this application, you will be able to:

1. Extend and record information on an inventory form.
2. Calculate the value of an inventory.
3. Calculate the potential profit of an inventory.

INSTRUCTIONS

Refer to the China Inventory form. Column 1 shows the inventory on the first day of the month. Column 2 shows the items purchased since the beginning of the month. Column 3 lists the number of items sold during the month. Column 5 shows the cost to the store for each item. Column 7 shows the price the store charges customers for each item. Complete the China Inventory form as follows (round answers to whole numbers):

1. To calculate the current inventory, add Purchases by Piece (Column 2) to Previous Inventory by Piece (Column 1) and subtract Number of Pieces Sold (Column 3). Record the result in Current Inventory by Piece (Column 4).

2. Multiply the Current Inventory by Piece (Column 4) by the Cost Per Piece (Column 5). Record the result in Total Cost of Inventory (Column 6).

3. To determine the retail value of the inventory, multiply the Current Inventory by Piece (Column 4) by the Retail Price Per Piece (Column 7). Record the result in Total Retail Value of Inventory (Column 8).

4. Calculate the potential profit by subtracting Total Cost of Inventory (Column 6) from Total Retail Value of Inventory (Column 8). Record the result in Potential Profit (Column 9).

5. Repeat Steps 1-4 for each inventory item listed in the Description column.

6. Total Columns 6, 8 and 9; write the total on each column's Total line.

7. Verify your calculations. The total of Column 6 subtracted from the total of Column 8 should match the total of Column 9.

CHINA INVENTORY

April 15, 20--

Description	1 Previous Inventory by Piece	2 Purchases by Piece	3 Number of Pieces Sold	4 Current Inventory by Piece	5 Cost Per Piece	6 Total Cost of Inventory	7 Retail Price Per Piece	8 Total Retail Value of Inventory	9 Potential Profit
Dinner Plate	809	132	451		$13	$	$33	$	$
Salad/Dessert Plate	725	216	213		9		26		
Butter Plate	413		64		7		18		
Cup & Saucer	934	7	512		19		55		
Soup/Salad Bowl	568				17		45		
Cream Soup & Stand	17	33	15		27		77		
Fruit/Dessert Saucer	210				12		32		
Demitasse Cup & Saucer	68	7	9		17		46		
Salad/Dessert Bowl	53	12	11		13		37		
Sauce Boat	10		3		56		149		
Buffet Platter	9		5		42		114		
Oval Platter 13"	15	4	12		45		122		
Oval Platter 15"	13		4		59		137		
Oval Platter 17"	6	6			65		159		
Round Platter 18"	7		2		72		175		
Open Vegetable - Large	17		15		38		103		
Open Vegetable - Small	21		8		27		77		
Covered Vegetable	12	8			86		236		
Oval Casserole – 3 qt.	23	12	11		78		217		
Round Casserole – 1.5 qt.	10				46		128		
Sugar Bowl	37	17	18		32		81		
Creamer	35	15	13		28		78		
Pepper Mill	27		5		15		32		
Salt Shaker	25	15	6		8		16		
Coffee Pot	16		4		58		149		
Totals									

Application 3-8
Update Office Supply Stock Inventory

OBJECTIVES

Upon completion of this application, you will be able to:

1. Calculate extensions.
2. Compute a discount.
3. Determine the cost of an inventory.

INSTRUCTIONS

The Warehouse Inventory form is divided into two sections by a heavy black line. Complete the left section first by following these steps:

1. Multiply the Quantity by the Price; write the Extension. (Round to two decimal places.) Follow this procedure for the entire section.

2. When you have completed the left section, follow the same procedure for the right section.

3. After calculating all extensions, add the figures in the Extension columns for both the left and right sections. Write the Total.

4. To calculate the amount of the discount, multiply the Total by 20%.

5. Subtract the amount of the discount from the Total. Write the Cost.

6. When you have completed the form, write your initials at the top of the form after the words Extended by.

When you have completed Unit 3, ask your teacher the procedure for submitting this unit. Do not begin Unit 4 until your teacher has approved Unit 3.

Office Supply Stock Inventory

6/30 20 -- 26

Called by ___E.J.___ Supplier ___J&R___ Priced by ___W.H.___

Sheet number

Entered by ___C.K.___ Location ___Dept. 972___ Extended by _____

ITEM	QUANTITY	PRICE	EXTENSION	ITEM	QUANTITY	PRICE	EXTENSION
Paper				**CD**			
Inkjet	152	$1.25	$	50 Pk CD-R Spindle	1,126	$ .49	$
Image Copy	237	2.75		100 Pk CD-R Spindle	187	1.49	
Photo Glossy	98	1.49		10 Pk CD-RW	91	.85	
Multipurpose	258	.79		12 Pk CD-RW	263	.89	
Laser	45	3.50		10 Pk DVD+ RW	794	1.15	
Recycled	115	.89		25 Pk DVD+ R	315	1.39	
Photo Matte	230	1.15		25 Pk 4.7 GB DVD	612	2.00	
White Copy	86	.69		100 Pk Jewel Cases	285	1.77	
Paper Clips				**File Folders**			
Jumbo	315	1.15		Poly-Expanding	405	1.79	
#2	68	.89		1/3 Cut Hanging 100-Pk	391	.89	
#2 Vinyl-Coated	105	1.39		Plastic 12-Pk	650	1.50	
Jumbo Vinyl	96	1.05		Manila 100-Pk	813	.79	
Envelopes				**Writing Instruments**			
24# No. 10 500 ct	231	1.35		12-Pk Highlighters	313	2.05	
24# No. 10 100 ct	117	.59		6-Pk Permanent Markers	54	1.49	
24# No. 9 500 ct	23	1.85		12-Pk Ballpoint Pens	806	.99	
24# No. 9 100 ct	846	2.50		Dry-Erase Markers	137	2.35	
24# No. 6 500 ct	312	2.75		Storage Boxes 4-Pk	11	12.35	
24# No. 6 100 ct	1,099	.59		Cordless Electric Stapler	18	17.50	
#37 Clasp	182	1.49		Desktop Printing Calculator	26	23.75	
#28 Clasp	144	1.98		High-Capacity Hole Punch	101	6.98	
#90 Clasp	83	3.15		Digital Coin Sorter	36	29.98	
9-V 2-Pk Batteries	209	2.85		Fire-Safe Security File	15	30.98	
AA 4-Pk Batteries	663	.79		Storage Cabinet with Sorter	37	24.98	

Total	$
Discount (20%)	$
Cost	$

Unit 3
Applications Evaluation

Last Name _____ First Name _____

Refer to completed Applications 3-1 through 3-8 to answer the following questions. The total point value of all the questions for each application as well as the point value of each individual question is indicated by the numbers in parentheses. Leave the Points Earned column blank. Your teacher will complete it.

Application 3-1

Points Earned

Complete Enrollment Reports (6) (2 each)

_____ of 6

How many majors had a 25% or higher decrease from 2004-2005? _____

What was the 2004 combined enrollment in Education, Liberal Arts, and Social Science majors? _____

What was the 2005 combined enrollment in Business, Engineering, Nursing, and Pharmacy majors? _____

Application 3-2

Determine Installment Buying Costs (6) (2 each)

_____ of 6

What was the total Cost of Borrowing for all 10 items? _____

What was the total Cost of Borrowing for all 36-month loans? _____

What was the total Cost of Borrowing for all 24-month loans? _____

Application 3-3

Prepare Departmental Expense Report (18) (3 each)

_____ of 18

What were the combined car mileage expenses for Allen, Cook, and Davis? _____

What were the combined meals and lodging expenses for Garrison, Parks, and Thompson? _____

What were the combined gratuities and other expenses for Boyle, Jensen, and Richards? _____

What were the combined transportation, meals, and lodging expenses for Thompson, West, and Zandy? _____

What were the combined total expenses for Boyle, Fuller, Mann, and Richards? _____

What were the combined meals, lodging, and other expenses for Ellis, Fuller, and Jensen? _____

Application 3-4

Calculate Fuel Amount Pumped (15) (3 each)

What were the total combined gallons pumped of Regular and Plus? _____

What were the total customers served buying Plus and Premium? _____

If Regular costs $1.54 per gallon, what were the total sales for Regular gasoline? _____

If Plus costs $1.67 per gallon, what were the total sales for Plus gasoline? _____

If Premium costs $1.75 per gallon, what were the total sales for Premium gasoline? _____

Application 3-5

Prepare Car Rental Contracts (18) (3 each)

What was the total combined amount for basic rental and hourly charges? _____

What was the total combined amount for gasoline and mileage charges? _____

Insurance charges accounted for what percent of the total charges (rounded to a whole number)? _____

What was the total of basic rental charges for those with government contracts? _____

What was the total of basic rental charges for those with corporate contracts? _____

Basic rental charges at the standard rate accounted for what percent of the total basic rental charges (rounded to a whole number)? _____

Application 3-6

Complete Linen Inventory (7) (Value beside each)

How many items were on hand at the beginning of the inventory period? (1) _____

What was the total number of items for which to be accounted? (1) _____

How many items were transferred to salvage? (1) _____

How many items were on hand at the end of the inventory period? (1) _____

What was the total number of loss items? (1) _____

For how many items was there no loss? (2) _____

Application 3-7

Calculate China Inventory (19) (Value beside each)

What was the total retail value of all inventory items? (1) _____

What was the total number of pieces in the previous inventory? (3) _____

What was the total number of pieces sold? (3) _____

What was the total number of pieces in the current inventory? (3) _____

What was the total retail value of all platters? (3) _____

What was the total retail value of all plates? (3) _____

What was the total retail value of all vegetable and casserole pieces? (3) _____

Application 3-8

Update Office Supply Stock Inventory (11) (Value beside each)

What was the total value of the inventory? (1)_____

What was the amount of the 20% discount? (1)_____

What was the total cost (after the discount)? (1)_____

What was the total quantity of all paper in stock? (2)_____

What was the total quantity of all CDs in stock? (2)_____

What was the total quantity of all Envelopes in stock? (2)_____

What was the total quantity of all File Folders in stock? (2)_____

Grading Scale

A = 100–94 points
B = 93–86 points
C = 85–78 points
D = 77–70 points

Total Points Earned of 100 _____

Unit 3 Applications Evaluation Grade _____

Petty Cash, Ledger Accounts, and Payroll

Name _____

Date Started _____

Date Completed _____

Unit 4 has 6 applications and requires approximately 250 minutes. Read the instructions carefully; do not seek help from your teacher until you have studied the instructions thoroughly. Estimate how much time to spend on each application and time your work to meet a deadline of 250 minutes. *Do not waste time.*

For each application, keep an accurate record of when you start and when you finish. Continue to verify your calculations.

When you have completed all 6 applications, ask your teacher the procedure for submitting this unit for approval.

 **Unit Four Time Record**

Application	Time Stopped	Time Started	Minutes Required
4-1			
4-2			
4-3			
4-4			
4-5			
4-6			
Total Minutes Required			

_____

Teacher's Approval

Application 4-1
Calculate Cash Drawer Funds

OBJECTIVES

Upon completion of this application, you will be able to:

1. Calculate the value of each denomination.
2. Calculate the total amount of funds in each cash drawer.
3. Calculate the grand total of funds in all cash drawers.

INSTRUCTIONS

Follow these steps to complete each Cash Drawer Count:

1. For each denomination, multiply the Count by the value of the denomination. For example, 416 x .05 (nickels) = 20.80. Write the result in the Amount column.
2. After completing the extensions for all coins and bills, add the Amount columns; write the result in the Total space.
3. Add the Totals of all three Cash Drawer Counts; write the result on the June 23, 20— Grand Total line.

CASH DRAWER COUNT

Date *June 23, 20--*
Time *3 a.m.*
Initials *WDB*

Denomination	Count	Amount
COINS		
Pennies	839	$
Nickels	558	
Dimes	782	
Quarters	545	
BILLS		
$1	865	
$5	438	
$10	271	
$20	137	
$50	10	
$100	2	
	Total	$

CASH DRAWER COUNT		
Date June 23, 20--		
Time 11 a.m.		
Initials BBC		

Denomination	Count	Amount
COINS		
Pennies	728	$
Nickels	447	
Dimes	671	
Quarters	434	
BILLS		
$1	754	
$5	327	
$10	160	
$20	207	
$50	23	
$100	4	
	Total	$

CASH DRAWER COUNT		
Date June 23, 20--		
Time 7 p.m.		
Initials QJS		

Denomination	Count	Amount
COINS		
Pennies	567	$
Nickels	345	
Dimes	390	
Quarters	421	
BILLS		
$1	938	
$5	274	
$10	483	
$20	196	
$50	37	
$100	8	
	Total	$

June 23, 20 -- Grand Total $ _____

Application 4-2
Prepare Petty Cash Record

Time Stopped _____

– Time Started _____

= Minutes Required _____

OBJECTIVES

Upon completion of this application, you will be able to:

1. Transfer data from petty cash vouchers to a petty cash record.
2. Calculate expenditures by date.
3. Calculate expenditures by category.

INSTRUCTIONS

Petty cash is money used to pay for items costing small amounts. Also, petty cash may be used for items needed quickly that require cash payment. A Petty Cash Voucher is completed each time petty cash is spent. A Petty Cash Record is kept detailing each expenditure from the petty cash fund.

Entries for the first fifteen days of the month have already been made on the Petty Cash Record. Continue to transfer the data from the vouchers to the Petty Cash Record by following these steps:

1. On the Petty Cash Voucher, locate the expense category written on the Charge to line. Locate the same expense category column on the Petty Cash Record. Write the voucher amount in the expense category column on the appropriate date line.

2. If two vouchers were written on the same date for the same category, add the two amounts and write only one total on the Petty Cash Record. Do not write two figures in the same space.

3. When you have transferred all data from the vouchers to the Petty Cash Record, add each line across; write the total in the Total column.

4. Add each column down; write the totals. Add the totals across to verify the sum of the Total column.

Amount $ 8.12
RECEIVED OF PETTY CASH
3/16/--
TO: Parcel Express
FOR: Parcel delivery service
CHARGE TO: Delivery Expense
R.g.B.   C.J.
Approved by   Received by

Amount $ 11.56
RECEIVED OF PETTY CASH
3/16/--
TO: Alex Cleaning Supplies
FOR: Cleaning supplies
CHARGE TO: Supplies Expense
R.g.B.   D.H.
Approved by   Received by

Amount $ 8.72
RECEIVED OF PETTY CASH
3/17/--
TO: M. Walters, Inc.
FOR: Warehouse locks
CHARGE TO: Warehouse Expense
R.g.B.   M.M.
Approved by   Received by

Amount $ 6.74
RECEIVED OF PETTY CASH
3/18/--
TO: Freeman Office Supply
FOR: Paper clips, tape
CHARGE TO: Office Expense
R.g.B.   M.B.J.
Approved by   Received by

Amount $ 15.00
RECEIVED OF PETTY CASH
3/18/--
TO: James Jester
FOR: Postage due
CHARGE TO: Postage Expense
R.g.B.   a.a.
Approved by   Received by

Amount $ 5.00
RECEIVED OF PETTY CASH
3/19/--
TO: Junior League Sports
FOR: Baseball donation
CHARGE TO: Miscellaneous Expense
R.g.B.   J.C.
Approved by   Received by

Amount $ 9.50 **RECEIVED OF PETTY CASH** 3/20/-- TO: United Chemicals, Inc FOR: Pest control CHARGE TO: Warehouse Expense R.g.B. H.g. Approved by Received by	Amount $ 5.45 **RECEIVED OF PETTY CASH** 3/20/-- TO: Freeman Office Supply FOR: Copier paper CHARGE TO: Office Expense R.g.B. M.B.J. Approved by Received by	Amount $ 8.35 **RECEIVED OF PETTY CASH** 3/22/-- TO: James Jester FOR: Postage due CHARGE TO: Postage Expense R.g.B. C.C. Approved by Received by
Amount $ 1.19 **RECEIVED OF PETTY CASH** 3/22/-- TO: Alex Cleaning Supplies FOR: Computer cleaner CHARGE TO: Supplies Expense R.g.B. D.H. Approved by Received by	Amount $ 7.26 **RECEIVED OF PETTY CASH** 3/23/-- TO: Federal Paint Stores FOR: Paint CHARGE TO: Supplies Expense R.g.B. P.Q. Approved by Received by	Amount $ 11.79 **RECEIVED OF PETTY CASH** 3/23/-- TO: Uptown Parcel Service FOR: Parcel delivery CHARGE TO: Delivery Expense R.g.B. C.J. Approved by Received by
Amount $ 5.00 **RECEIVED OF PETTY CASH** 3/24/-- TO: Athletic Booster Club FOR: Donation CHARGE TO: Miscellaneous Expense R.g.B. g.M. Approved by Received by	Amount $ 5.75 **RECEIVED OF PETTY CASH** 3/24/-- TO: Tri-Cities Electrical Corp. FOR: Wiring CHARGE TO: Warehouse Expense R.g.B. P.C. Approved by Received by	Amount $ 3.75 **RECEIVED OF PETTY CASH** 3/24/-- TO: Jiffy Jones Repair Service FOR: Laptop computer case repair CHARGE TO: Office Expense R.g.B. B.H. Approved by Received by
Amount $ 22.30 **RECEIVED OF PETTY CASH** 3/25/-- TO: Roundtown Delivery FOR: Parcel delivery service CHARGE TO: Delivery Expense R.g.B. C.J. Approved by Received by	Amount $ 10.00 **RECEIVED OF PETTY CASH** 3/26/-- TO: Thomasville HS FOR: Program ad CHARGE TO: Miscellaneous Expense R.g.B. S.W. Approved by Received by	Amount $ 9.45 **RECEIVED OF PETTY CASH** 3/26/-- TO: Alex Cleaning Supplies FOR: Ink remover CHARGE TO: Supplies Expense R.g.B. D.H. Approved by Received by
Amount $ 8.09 **RECEIVED OF PETTY CASH** 3/27/-- TO: Salem Hardware Co. FOR: Picture hangers CHARGE TO: Supplies Expense R.g.B. R.Y. Approved by Received by	Amount $ 12.16 **RECEIVED OF PETTY CASH** 3/27/-- TO: Tucker Trucking Lines FOR: Delivery service CHARGE TO: Delivery Expense R.g.B. L.L.D. Approved by Received by	Amount $ 11.90 **RECEIVED OF PETTY CASH** 3/27/-- TO: Leon Little Lumber Co. FOR: Window repairs CHARGE TO: Warehouse Expense R.g.B. R.B. Approved by Received by

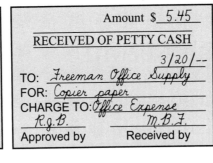
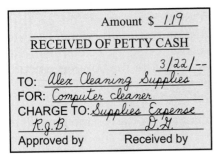
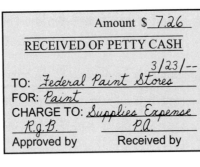
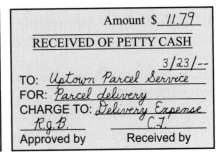

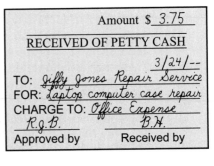
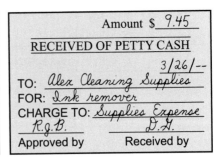
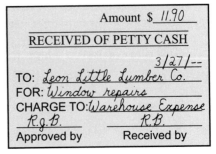

Amount $ 7.36

RECEIVED OF PETTY CASH

3/29/--

TO: James Jester

FOR: Postage due

CHARGE TO: Postage Expense

R.g.B.   C.C.

Approved by   Received by

Amount $ 3.83

RECEIVED OF PETTY CASH

3/29/--

TO: Freeman Office Supply

FOR: Copier service

CHARGE TO: Office Expense

R.g.B.   M.B.F.

Approved by   Received by

Amount $ 15.00

RECEIVED OF PETTY CASH

3/30/--

TO: Postmaster

FOR: Stamps

CHARGE TO: Postage Expense

R.g.B.   C.C.

Approved by   Received by

Amount $ 11.35

RECEIVED OF PETTY CASH

3/30/--

TO: Salem Hardware Co.

FOR: Caulk

CHARGE TO: Office Expense

R.g.B.   B.g.V.

Approved by   Received by

Amount $ 13.89

RECEIVED OF PETTY CASH

3/30/--

TO: Regent Chemical Corp.

FOR: Air freshener

CHARGE TO: Supplies Expense

R.g.B.   A.C.

Approved by   Received by

Amount $ 6.29

RECEIVED OF PETTY CASH

3/30/--

TO: Freeman Office Supply

FOR: Fine-point pens

CHARGE TO: Office Expense

R.g.B.   P.W.

Approved by   Received by

Amount $ 12.59

RECEIVED OF PETTY CASH

3/31/--

TO: Freeman Office Supply

FOR: Calculator machine tape

CHARGE TO: Office Expense

R.g.B.   M.B.F.

Approved by   Received by

Amount $ 4.50

RECEIVED OF PETTY CASH

3/31/--

TO: About Town Cab

FOR: Taxi

CHARGE TO: Miscellaneous Expense

R.g.B.   E.E.C.

Approved by   Received by

Amount $ 10.65

RECEIVED OF PETTY CASH

3/31/--

TO: Roundtown Delivery

FOR: Parcel delivery service

CHARGE TO: Delivery Expense

R.g.B.   C.J.

Approved by   Received by

PETTY CASH RECORD

Date	Office Expense	Supplies Expense	Delivery Expense	Warehouse Expense	Postage Expense	Miscellaneous Expense	Total
3/1	$	$	$ 6.40	$	$ 15.00	$ 8.58	$
3/2	12.80						
3/3		8.52		1.46		3.09	
3/4	8.20		3.30		.97		
3/5	11.75	3.92				12.16	
3/6		10.06		8.60			
3/8	16.49	3.51			1.35	5.00	
3/9		2.80	15.45			.39	
3/10	1.38		7.80				
3/11	6.70			9.45		2.25	
3/12		11.56			3.05	2.25	
3/13	5.12						
3/15			8.50				
3/16							
3/17							
3/18							
3/19							
3/20							
3/22							
3/23							
3/24							
3/25							
3/26							
3/27							
3/29							
3/30							
3/31							
Total	$	$	$	$	$	$	$

Application 4-3
Balance Ledger Accounts

OBJECTIVE

Upon completion of this application, you will be able to calculate customer account balances in individual ledger accounts.

INSTRUCTIONS

A ledger account is a record of the amounts charged to a customer's account and the amounts paid on their account. The balance of the account is always shown in the last column. Charges to an account are added to the balance. Payments to an account are subtracted from the balance.

When merchandise is returned or a payment is made for an amount that is more than the balance, the account will have a credit balance. On the calculator or computer screen, you may see a minus sign or a CR that indicates a credit balance.

Complete each ledger account line by line as follows (the first ledger has been completed for you):

1. Add any January 1 balance. Subtract any CR (credit) balance.

2. Add figures in the Charges (+) column to the Balance; subtotal; write the result in the Balance column.

3. Subtract figures in the Payments (-) column from the Balance; subtotal; write the result in the Balance column.

4. Write CR beside any amount resulting in a credit balance in the Balance column.

5. At the end of the ledger account, obtain an ending balance; write the result in the Balance column.

NAME Allbutton, Inc. ACCOUNT NO. 1139
ADDRESS P.O. Box 4023, Santa Ana, CA 92702-6528

DATE 20--		+ CHARGES	– PAYMENTS	BALANCE
Jan	1			7 8 90
	27	1 1 1 85		1 9 0 75
Feb	5		1 9 0 75	0
	14	1 5 9 80		1 5 9 80
	20	6 3 93		2 2 3 73
	25	1 5 57		2 3 9 30
Mar	3		2 0 8 91	3 0 39
	19		3 0 39	0

NAME Billie Jean and Doris's Dress Shop **ACCOUNT NO.** 2045

ADDRESS 323 Onyx Drive, Santa Ana, CA 92704-4431

DATE 20--			+ CHARGES	− PAYMENTS	BALANCE
Jan	1				0
Feb	1		66 87		
	5		132 48		
	20		29 97		
Mar	4			229 23	
	8		211 45		
	19		65 47		
	28			200 00	

NAME Crenshaw & McLemore, Inc. **ACCOUNT NO.** 3705

ADDRESS 2525 King Charles Drive, Austin, TX 78724-7289

DATE 20--			+ CHARGES	− PAYMENTS	BALANCE
Jan	1				181 09
	18		60 69		
	31		121 65		
Feb	5		44 35		
	9			400 00	
	20		38 89		
	25		211 56		
Mar	3			200 00	

NAME Farmer and Marshall Corp. **ACCOUNT NO.** 6390

ADDRESS 8216 South Gaucho St. Mesa, AZ 85202-5137

DATE 20--			+ CHARGES	− PAYMENTS	BALANCE
Jan	1				0
	6		25 30		
Feb	5		67 89		
	7		139 60		
	14			230 00	
	26		82 55		
Mar	2			100 00	
	18		206 45		

NAME Lyon, Chapman, and Saunders   ACCOUNT NO. 10348

ADDRESS 8181 Autumn Drive, Anaheim, CA 92805-7928

DATE 20--			+ CHARGES	− PAYMENTS	BALANCE
Jan	1				246 87
	11		35 19		
Feb	2			282 06	
	17		343 80		
	26		48 35		
Mar	3			400 00	
	11		71 39		
	30			63 54	

NAME McDowell and McDowell, Inc.   ACCOUNT NO. 11824

ADDRESS 2060 Greenbrier Rd., Santa Ana, CA 92705-3566

DATE 20--			+ CHARGES	− PAYMENTS	BALANCE
Jan	1				8 98
	20		47 09		
Feb	1		100 36		
	2			156 00	
Mar	4		5 28		
	9		38 54		
	18		262 75		
	27			300 00	

NAME O'Daniel and Sons, Inc.   ACCOUNT NO. 12037

ADDRESS P.O. Box 11678, Santa Ana, CA 92711-8625

DATE 20--			+ CHARGES	− PAYMENTS	BALANCE
Jan	1				17 75
	9		26 88		
Feb	2			44 63	
Mar	2		335 76		
	11		60 96		
	21		14 58		
	23			400 00	
	30		82 74		

NAME Steinbaugh and Hoskinson, Inc. **ACCOUNT NO.** 16492

ADDRESS 1628 East 17th St., Santa Ana, CA 92701-6519

DATE 20--			+ CHARGES	− PAYMENTS	BALANCE
Jan	1				1578 CR
Feb	5		12378		
	9		5689		
	16			16500	
	20		6497		
Mar	1		13645		
	19		870		
	30			21000	

NAME Styles by Tillie **ACCOUNT NO.** 16720

ADDRESS 327 Lemon Leaf Lane, Santa Ana, CA 92705-3781

DATE 20--			+ CHARGES	− PAYMENTS	BALANCE
Jan	1				1245
	6		2850		
Feb	2			4095	
	16		13974		
Mar	5			14000	
	15		3156		
	17		10735		
	31			14000	

NAME Tannenbaum Brothers, Inc. **ACCOUNT NO.** 17730

ADDRESS 1823 12th St., Sacramento, CA 92507-7566

DATE 20--			+ CHARGES	− PAYMENTS	BALANCE
Jan	1				15995
	12		7995		
	15			10000	
Feb	3		18870		
	15			15000	
Mar	4		6445		
	11		3778	20000	
	18		2220		

NAME United Markets, Inc. ACCOUNT NO. 18829
ADDRESS 1110 Wilshire Blvd., Los Angeles, CA 90017-9312

DATE 20--			+ CHARGES	− PAYMENTS	BALANCE
Jan	1				——0——
	10		145 35		
	26		28 25		
Feb	1		90 56		
	10			264 16	
	20		32 30		
Mar	1		49 45		
	19		18 39		

NAME Wagoner, Davis, Parker, & Fox, Inc. ACCOUNT NO. 20104
ADDRESS 3827 North Central Avenue, Phoenix, AZ 85012-2793

DATE 20--			+ CHARGES	− PAYMENTS	BALANCE
Jan	1				202 65
	3		139 46		
	11			342 00	
	19		58 50		
Feb	6		313 79		
Mar	2			375 00	
	12		72 25		
	30		21 45		

NAME Kountry Klassics Designs ACCOUNT NO. 20390
ADDRESS 241 Mendal Pkwy, San Jose, CA 95112-9728

DATE 20--			+ CHARGES	− PAYMENTS	BALANCE
Jan	1				426 78
	12		53 91		
Feb	5			228.60	
	15		438 30		
	24		84 53		
Mar	6			500.00	
	12		17 93		
	29			56.43	

NAME Compos-It Concepts, Inc.		ACCOUNT NO. 20395				
ADDRESS 611 Interstate Park, San Jose, CA 95112-9728						

DATE 20--		+ CHARGES	− PAYMENTS	BALANCE
Jan	1			264.89
	13	93.51		
Feb	6		128.50	
	13	381.20		
	20	48.75		
Mar	7		225.00	
	14	71.39		
	28		506.24	

158

Application 4-4

Prepare Biweekly Payroll Record

OBJECTIVES

Upon completion of this application, you will be able to:

1. Calculate FICA and state income tax withholdings.
2. Read tax charts to determine federal income tax withholdings.
3. Total deductions.
4. Calculate net earnings.
5. Complete a payroll record.

INSTRUCTIONS

Follow these steps to complete the Biweekly Payroll Record:

1. Calculate the FICA tax (Federal Insurance Contributions Act, also known as Social Security) (Column 1) for each employee by multiplying the Biweekly Salary by 7.65%. If you have a percent key, use it. If not, multiply by .0765. Round to two decimal places.

2. Determine the federal income tax to be withheld for each employee by referring to the tax table for Single Persons or the tax table for Married Persons. The Dependents (Column 2) on the Payroll Record indicates the table to be used and the number of dependents. For example, M-2 means married with two dependents and S-1 means single with one dependent. Refer to the tax tables. On the tax table for Married Persons, look at the column heading *If the wages are—* with the subheadings *At least* and *But less than*. If the salary is $1,490, read down the *If the wages are* column to the line

   At least 1,480 *But less than* 1,500, then read across the column heading *And the number of withholding allowances claimed is—*. A person with a biweekly salary of $1,490, married claiming two dependents (M-2) would have $114 a month withheld for federal income tax (Column 3).

3. If a single person's salary exceeds $2,100 or a married person's salary exceeds $2,700, follow the Percentage Method for calculating the person's federal income taxes.

4. State income tax (Column 4) is based on the amount of federal income tax withheld, not on salary. Calculate state income tax to be withheld for each employee by multiplying the federal income tax withheld by 23% (.23).

5. When you have calculated each employee's FICA, Federal, and State Income Tax withholdings, follow this procedure to calculate the Net Earnings for each employee.

   a. Add all deductions (Column 1 and Columns 3-6) for each employee. Write the result in the Total Deductions column.

   b. Subtract Total Deductions from the Biweekly Salary for each employee; write the result in the Net Earnings column.

6. When you have calculated the Net Earnings for each employee, calculate the column totals on the Payroll Record.

7. Verify your calculations. The Biweekly Salary total minus the Total Deductions total should match the Net Earnings total. Also, the totals of Column 1 and Columns 3–6 should equal the Total Deductions total.

CONTINENTAL DISTRIBUTORS, INC.

PAYROLL RECORD for the period of _February 1–14, 20—_

Employee (Last Name, Initials)	Biweekly Salary	FICA Tax¹	Depen- dents²	Income Tax Federal³	State⁴	Credit Union⁵	Company Mdse.⁶	Total Deductions	Net Earnings
Vickery, V. A.	$ 1,395.00	$	S–0	$	$	$ 25.00	$ 9.00	$	$
Stogner, I. C.	1,475.00		S–1			35.00	8.00		
Peace, M. W.	1,523.00		M–0			50.00	3.00		
Perez, B. R.	1,620.00		S–1			35.00	5.00		
O'Konley, C.O.	1,750.00		S–2			20.00	5.00		
Nelson, H. H.	1,859.00		M–6			15.00	40.00		
McKenzie, O. B.	1,972.00		S–1			25.00	5.00		
Kovach, J. M.	2,012.00		S–1			50.00	10.00		
Huff, N. J.	2,175.00		M–4			50.00	12.00		
Granger, D. E.	2,349.00		M–1			10.00	0		
Torres, W. W.	2,520.00		M–3			75.00	15.00		
Disharoon, B. W.	2,860.00		S–3			100.00	35.00		
Conway, A. B.	3,215.00		M–2			150.00	45.00		
Alverez, C.J.	3,530.00		M–5			125.00	50.00		
Total	$	$		$	$	$	$	$	$

SINGLE Persons—BIWEEKLY Payroll Period

(For Wages Paid Through December 20--)

If the wages are—		And the number of withholding allowances claimed is—										
At least	But less than	0	1	2	3	4	5	6	7	8	9	10
		The amount of income tax to be withheld is—										
$800	$820	$93	$75	$57	$39	$23	$11	$0	$0	$0	$0	$0
820	840	96	78	60	42	25	13	1	0	0	0	0
840	860	99	81	63	45	27	15	3	0	0	0	0
860	880	102	84	66	48	30	17	5	0	0	0	0
880	900	105	87	69	51	33	19	7	0	0	0	0
900	920	108	90	72	54	36	21	9	0	0	0	0
920	940	111	93	75	57	39	23	11	0	0	0	0
940	960	114	96	78	60	42	25	13	1	0	0	0
960	980	117	99	81	63	45	27	15	3	0	0	0
980	1,000	120	102	84	66	48	30	17	5	0	0	0
1,000	1,020	123	105	87	69	51	33	19	7	0	0	0
1,020	1,040	126	108	90	72	54	36	21	9	0	0	0
1,040	1,060	129	111	93	75	57	39	23	11	0	0	0
1,060	1,080	132	114	96	78	60	42	25	13	1	0	0
1,080	1,100	135	117	99	81	63	45	27	15	3	0	0
1,100	1,120	138	120	102	84	66	48	30	17	5	0	0
1,120	1,140	141	123	105	87	69	51	33	19	7	0	0
1,140	1,160	144	126	108	90	72	54	36	21	9	0	0
1,160	1,180	147	129	111	93	75	57	39	23	11	0	0
1,180	1,200	150	132	114	96	78	60	42	25	13	2	0
1,200	1,220	155	135	117	99	81	63	45	27	15	4	0
1,220	1,240	160	138	120	102	84	66	48	30	17	6	0
1,240	1,260	165	141	123	105	87	69	51	33	19	8	0
1,260	1,280	170	144	126	108	90	72	54	36	21	10	0
1,280	1,300	175	147	129	111	93	75	57	39	23	12	0
1,300	1,320	180	150	132	114	96	78	60	42	25	14	2
1,320	1,340	185	155	135	117	99	81	63	45	28	16	4
1,340	1,360	190	160	138	120	102	84	66	48	31	18	6
1,360	1,380	195	165	141	123	105	87	69	51	34	20	8
1,380	1,400	200	170	144	126	108	90	72	54	37	22	10
1,400	1,420	205	175	147	129	111	93	75	57	40	24	12
1,420	1,440	210	180	151	132	114	96	78	60	43	26	14
1,440	1,460	215	185	156	135	117	99	81	63	46	28	16
1,460	1,480	220	190	161	138	120	102	84	66	49	31	18
1,480	1,500	225	195	166	141	123	105	87	69	52	34	20
1,500	1,520	230	200	171	144	126	108	90	72	55	37	22
1,520	1,540	235	205	176	147	129	111	93	75	58	40	24
1,540	1,560	240	210	181	151	132	114	96	78	61	43	26
1,560	1,580	245	215	186	156	135	117	99	81	64	46	28
1,580	1,600	250	220	191	161	138	120	102	84	67	49	31
1,600	1,620	255	225	196	166	141	123	105	87	70	52	34
1,620	1,640	260	230	201	171	144	126	108	90	73	55	37
1,640	1,660	265	235	206	176	147	129	111	93	76	58	40
1,660	1,680	270	240	211	181	151	132	114	96	79	61	43
1,680	1,700	275	245	216	186	156	135	117	99	82	64	46
1,700	1,720	280	250	221	191	161	138	120	102	85	67	49
1,720	1,740	285	255	226	196	166	141	123	105	88	70	52
1,740	1,760	290	260	231	201	171	144	126	108	91	73	55
1,760	1,780	295	265	236	206	176	147	129	111	94	76	58
1,780	1,800	300	270	241	211	181	151	132	114	97	79	61
1,800	1,820	305	275	246	216	186	156	135	117	100	82	64
1,820	1,840	310	280	251	221	191	161	138	120	103	85	67
1,840	1,860	315	285	256	226	196	166	141	123	106	88	70
1,860	1,880	320	290	261	231	201	171	144	126	109	91	73
1,880	1,900	325	295	266	236	206	176	147	129	112	94	76
1,900	1,920	330	300	271	241	211	181	151	132	115	97	79
1,920	1,940	335	305	276	246	216	186	156	135	118	100	82
1,940	1,960	340	310	281	251	221	191	161	138	121	103	85
1,960	1,980	345	315	286	256	226	196	166	141	124	106	88
1,980	2,000	350	320	291	261	231	201	171	144	127	109	91
2,000	2,020	355	325	296	266	236	206	176	147	130	112	94
2,020	2,040	360	330	301	271	241	211	181	152	133	115	97
2,040	2,060	365	335	306	276	246	216	186	157	136	118	100
2,060	2,080	370	340	311	281	251	221	191	162	139	121	103
2,080	2,100	375	345	316	286	256	226	196	167	142	124	106

$2,100 and over   Use Table 2(a) for a **SINGLE person** on page 164. Also see the instructions on page 163.

MARRIED Persons—BIWEEKLY Payroll Period
(For Wages Paid Through December 20--)

If the wages are—		And the number of withholding allowances claimed is—										
At least	But less than	0	1	2	3	4	5	6	7	8	9	10
		The amount of income tax to be withheld is—										
$1,380	$1,400	$135	$117	$99	$81	$63	$49	$37	$25	$13	$1	$0
1,400	1,420	138	120	102	84	66	51	39	27	15	3	0
1,420	1,440	141	123	105	87	69	53	41	29	17	5	0
1,440	1,460	144	126	108	90	72	55	43	31	19	7	0
1,460	1,480	147	129	111	93	75	57	45	33	21	9	0
1,480	1,500	150	132	114	96	78	60	47	35	23	11	0
1,500	1,520	153	135	117	99	81	63	49	37	25	13	1
1,520	1,540	156	138	120	102	84	66	51	39	27	15	3
1,540	1,560	159	141	123	105	87	69	53	41	29	17	5
1,560	1,580	162	144	126	108	90	72	55	43	31	19	7
1,580	1,600	165	147	129	111	93	75	58	45	33	21	9
1,600	1,620	168	150	132	114	96	78	61	47	35	23	11
1,620	1,640	171	153	135	117	99	81	64	49	37	25	13
1,640	1,660	174	156	138	120	102	84	67	51	39	27	15
1,660	1,680	177	159	141	123	105	87	70	53	41	29	17
1,680	1,700	180	162	144	126	108	90	73	55	43	31	19
1,700	1,720	183	165	147	129	111	93	76	58	45	33	21
1,720	1,740	186	168	150	132	114	96	79	61	47	35	23
1,740	1,760	189	171	153	135	117	99	82	64	49	37	25
1,760	1,780	192	174	156	138	120	102	85	67	51	39	27
1,780	1,800	195	177	159	141	123	105	88	70	53	41	29
1,800	1,820	198	180	162	144	126	108	91	73	55	43	31
1,820	1,840	201	183	165	147	129	111	94	76	58	45	33
1,840	1,860	204	186	168	150	132	114	97	79	61	47	35
1,860	1,880	207	189	171	153	135	117	100	82	64	49	37
1,880	1,900	210	192	174	156	138	120	103	85	67	51	39
1,900	1,920	213	195	177	159	141	123	106	88	70	53	41
1,920	1,940	216	198	180	162	144	126	109	91	73	55	43
1,940	1,960	219	201	183	165	147	129	112	94	76	58	45
1,960	1,980	222	204	186	168	150	132	115	97	79	61	47
1,980	2,000	225	207	189	171	153	135	118	100	82	64	49
2,000	2,020	228	210	192	174	156	138	121	103	85	67	51
2,020	2,040	231	213	195	177	159	141	124	106	88	70	53
2,040	2,060	234	216	198	180	162	144	127	109	91	73	55
2,060	2,080	237	219	201	183	165	147	130	112	94	76	58
2,080	2,100	240	222	204	186	168	150	133	115	97	79	61
2,100	2,120	243	225	207	189	171	153	136	118	100	82	64
2,120	2,140	246	228	210	192	174	156	139	121	103	85	67
2,140	2,160	249	231	213	195	177	159	142	124	106	88	70
2,160	2,180	252	234	216	198	180	162	145	127	109	91	73
2,180	2,200	255	237	219	201	183	165	148	130	112	94	76
2,200	2,220	258	240	222	204	186	168	151	133	115	97	79
2,220	2,240	261	243	225	207	189	171	154	136	118	100	82
2,240	2,260	264	246	228	210	192	174	157	139	121	103	85
2,260	2,280	267	249	231	213	195	177	160	142	124	106	88
2,280	2,300	270	252	234	216	198	180	163	145	127	109	91
2,300	2,320	273	255	237	219	201	183	166	148	130	112	94
2,320	2,340	276	258	240	222	204	186	169	151	133	115	97
2,340	2,360	279	261	243	225	207	189	172	154	136	118	100
2,360	2,380	282	264	246	228	210	192	175	157	139	121	103
2,380	2,400	285	267	249	231	213	195	178	160	142	124	106
2,400	2,420	288	270	252	234	216	198	181	163	145	127	109
2,420	2,440	291	273	255	237	219	201	184	166	148	130	112
2,440	2,460	294	276	258	240	222	204	187	169	151	133	115
2,460	2,480	297	279	261	243	225	207	190	172	154	136	118
2,480	2,500	300	282	264	246	228	210	193	175	157	139	121
2,500	2,520	305	285	267	249	231	213	196	178	160	142	124
2,520	2,540	310	288	270	252	234	216	199	181	163	145	127
2,540	2,560	315	291	273	255	237	219	202	184	166	148	130
2,560	2,580	320	294	276	258	240	222	205	187	169	151	133
2,580	2,600	325	297	279	261	243	225	208	190	172	154	136
2,600	2,620	330	300	282	264	246	228	211	193	175	157	139
2,620	2,640	335	305	285	267	249	231	214	196	178	160	142
2,640	2,660	340	310	288	270	252	234	217	199	181	163	145
2,660	2,680	345	315	291	273	255	237	220	202	184	166	148
2,680	2,700	350	320	294	276	258	240	223	205	187	169	151

$2,700 and over Use Table 2(b) for a **MARRIED person** on page 164. Also see the instructions on page 163.

How To Use the Income Tax Withholding Payment Tables

Income Tax Withholding

There are several ways to figure income tax withholding. The following methods of withholding are based on information that you get from your employees on **Form W-4**, Employeeís Withholding Allowance Certificate.

Wage Bracket Method

Under the wage bracket method, find the proper table (on pages 5-24) for your payroll period and the employeeís marital status as shown on his or her Form W-4. Then, based on the number of withholding allowances claimed on the Form W-4 and the amount of wages, find the amount of tax to withhold. If your employee is claiming more than 10 withholding allowances, see below.

Note: If you cannot use the wage bracket tables because wages exceed the amount shown in the last bracket of the table, use the percentage method of withholding described below. Be sure to reduce wages by the amount of total withholding allowances in Table 1 before using the percentage method tables (pages 3-4).

Adjusting wage bracket withholding for employees claiming more than 10 withholding allowances. The wage bracket tables can be used if an employee claims up to 10 allowances. More than 10 allowances may be claimed because of the special withholding allowance, additional allowances for deductions and credits, and the system itself.

To adapt the tables to more than 10 allowances:

1) Multiply the number of withholding allowances over 10 by the allowance value for the payroll period. (The allowance values are in **Table 1, Percentage Method—Amount for One Withholding Allowance** below.)

2) Subtract the result from the employeeís wages.

3) On this amount, find and withhold the tax in the column for 10 allowances.

This is a voluntary method. If you use the wage bracket tables, you may continue to withhold the amount in the ì10î column when your employee has more than 10 allowances, using the method above. You can also use any other method described below.

Percentage Method

If you do not want to use the wage bracket tables on pages 5 through 24 to figure how much income tax to withhold, you can use a percentage computation based on Table 1 and the appropriate rate table. This method works for any number of withholding allowances that the employee claims and any amount of wages.

Use these steps to figure the income tax to withhold under the Percentage Method:

1) Multiply one withholding allowance for your payroll period (see **Table 1** below) by the number of allowances that the employee claims.

2) Subtract that amount from the employeeís wages.

3) Determine the amount to withhold from the appropriate table on page 3 or 4.

Table 1. Percentage Method—Amount for One Withholding Allowance

Payroll Period	One Withholding Allowance
Weekly	$59.62
Biweekly	119.23
Semimonthly	129.17
Monthly	258.33
Quarterly	775.00
Semiannually	1,550.00
Annually	3,100.00
Daily or miscellaneous (each day of the payroll period)	11.92

Example: An unmarried employee is paid $600 weekly. This employee has in effect a Form W-4 claiming two withholding allowances. Using the Percentage Method, figure the income tax to withhold as follows:

1.	Total wage payment	$600.00
2.	One allowance	$59.62
3.	Allowances claimed on Form W-4	2
4.	Multiply line 2 by line 3	$119.24
5.	Amount subject to withholding (subtract line 4 from line 1)	$480.76
6.	Tax to be withheld on $480.76 from Table 1—single person, page 3	$57.66

To figure the income tax to withhold, you may reduce the last digit of the wages to zero, or figure the wages to the nearest dollar.

Alternative Methods of Income Tax Withholding

Rather than the Percentage Method or Wage Bracket Method, you can use an alternative method to withhold income tax. See page 25 for more information.

Whole-Dollar Withholding (Rounding)

The income tax withholding amounts in the Wage Bracket Tables (pages 5-24) have been rounded to whole-dollar amounts.

When employers use the Percentage Method (pages 3-4) or an alternative method of income tax withholding, the tax for the pay period may be rounded to the nearest dollar.

Tables for Percentage Method of Withholding
(For Wages Paid Through December 20--)

TABLE 1—WEEKLY Payroll Period

(a) SINGLE person (including head of household)—

If the amount of wages (after subtracting withholding allowances) is: The amount of income tax to withhold is:

Not over $51 . . . . . $0

Over—	But not over—		of excess over—
$51	—$187	10%	—$51
$187	—$592	$13.60 plus 15%	—$187
$592	—$1,317	$74.35 plus 25%	—$592
$1,317	—$2,860	$255.60 plus 28%	—$1,317
$2,860	—$6,177	$687.64 plus 33%	—$2,860
$6,177	. . . . . .	$1,782.25 plus 35%	—$6,177

(b) MARRIED person—

If the amount of wages (after subtracting withholding allowances) is: The amount of income tax to withhold is:

Not over $154 . . . . . $0

Over—	But not over—		of excess over—
$154	—$429	10%	—$154
$429	—$1,245	$27.50 plus 15%	—$429
$1,245	—$2,270	$149.90 plus 25%	—$1,245
$2,270	—$3,568	$406.15 plus 28%	—$2,270
$3,568	—$6,271	$769.59 plus 33%	—$3,568
$6,271	. . . . . .	$1,661.58 plus 35%	—$6,271

TABLE 2—BIWEEKLY Payroll Period

(a) SINGLE person (including head of household)—

If the amount of wages (after subtracting withholding allowances) is: The amount of income tax to withhold is:

Not over $102 . . . . . $0

Over—	But not over—		of excess over—
$102	—$373	10%	—$102
$373	—$1,185	$27.10 plus 15%	—$373
$1,185	—$2,635	$148.90 plus 25%	—$1,185
$2,635	—$5,719	$511.40 plus 28%	—$2,635
$5,719	—$12,354	$1,374.92 plus 33%	—$5,719
$12,354	. . . . . .	$3,564.47 plus 35%	—$12,354

(b) MARRIED person—

If the amount of wages (after subtracting withholding allowances) is: The amount of income tax to withhold is:

Not over $308 . . . . . $0

Over—	But not over—		of excess over—
$308	—$858	10%	—$308
$858	—$2,490	$55.00 plus 15%	—$858
$2,490	—$4,540	$299.80 plus 25%	—$2,490
$4,540	—$7,137	$812.30 plus 28%	—$4,540
$7,137	—$12,542	$1,539.46 plus 33%	—$7,137
$12,542	. . . . . .	$3,323.11 plus 35%	—$12,542

TABLE 3—SEMIMONTHLY Payroll Period

(a) SINGLE person (including head of household)—

If the amount of wages (after subtracting withholding allowances) is: The amount of income tax to withhold is:

Not over $110 . . . . . $0

Over—	But not over—		of excess over—
$110	—$404	10%	—$110
$404	—$1,283	$29.40 plus 15%	—$404
$1,283	—$2,854	$161.25 plus 25%	—$1,283
$2,854	—$6,196	$554.00 plus 28%	—$2,854
$6,196	—$13,383	$1,489.76 plus 33%	—$6,196
$13,383	. . . . . .	$3,861.47 plus 35%	—$13,383

(b) MARRIED person—

If the amount of wages (after subtracting withholding allowances) is: The amount of income tax to withhold is:

Not over $333 . . . . . $0

Over—	But not over—		of excess over—
$333	—$929	10%	—$333
$929	—$2,698	$59.60 plus 15%	—$929
$2,698	—$4,919	$324.95 plus 25%	—$2,698
$4,919	—$7,731	$880.20 plus 28%	—$4,919
$7,731	—$13,588	$1,667.56 plus 33%	—$7,731
$13,588	. . . . . .	$3,600.37 plus 35%	—$13,588

TABLE 4—MONTHLY Payroll Period

(a) SINGLE person (including head of household)—

If the amount of wages (after subtracting withholding allowances) is: The amount of income tax to withhold is:

Not over $221 . . . . . $0

Over—	But not over—		of excess over—
$221	—$808	10%	—$221
$808	—$2,567	$58.70 plus 15%	—$808
$2,567	—$5,708	$322.55 plus 25%	—$2,567
$5,708	—$12,392	$1,107.80 plus 28%	—$5,708
$12,392	—$26,767	$2,979.32 plus 33%	—$12,392
$26,767	. . . . . .	$7,723.07 plus 35%	—$26,767

(b) MARRIED person—

If the amount of wages (after subtracting withholding allowances) is: The amount of income tax to withhold is:

Not over $667 . . . . . $0

Over—	But not over—		of excess over—
$667	—$1,858	10%	—$667
$1,858	—$5,396	$119.10 plus 15%	—$1,858
$5,396	—$9,838	$649.80 plus 25%	—$5,396
$9,838	—$15,463	$1,760.30 plus 28%	—$9,838
$15,463	—$27,175	$3,335.30 plus 33%	—$15,463
$27,175	. . . . . .	$7,200.26 plus 35%	—$27,175

Application 4-5
Calculate Weekly Payroll

OBJECTIVES

Upon completion of this application, you will be able to:

1. Determine regular, overtime, and total earnings.

2. Complete individual time cards.

3. Transfer data and complete a payroll register.

4. Calculate FICA and state income tax withholdings.

5. Read tax charts to determine federal income tax withholdings.

6. Calculate total deductions and net pay.

INSTRUCTIONS

To complete the individual Time Cards, follow these steps to determine how the first Time Card was completed:

1. Calculate the total hours worked during the week by adding the Hours on each employee's Time Card. An excess of 8 hours a day is not considered overtime; however, total weekly hours over 40 are considered overtime. (On Alice Abel's Time Card, the Hours total 45. Alice worked 40 regular hours and 5 overtime hours.)

2. Calculate each employee's earnings:

   a. Multiply regular hours by the Hourly Rate shown on the Time Card. (For Alice, $9.50 x 40 = $380.00.)

   b. For hours worked beyond 40, multiply the Hourly Rate by 1.5 by the number of overtime hours. (For Alice, $9.50 x 1.5 = 14.25 (overtime rate) x 5 hours = $71.25.) You do not need to calculate the overtime rate if no overtime was worked.

   c. Calculate total earnings by adding the regular and overtime earnings. (For Alice, $380.00 + $71.25 = $451.25.)

3. Complete the remaining Time Cards by following the procedures given in Steps 1 and 2.

After you have completed all Time Cards, complete the Payroll Register as follows (the first line has been completed for you):

1. Transfer the total earnings from each Time Card to the Total Earnings column of the Payroll Register.

2. Calculate the FICA tax deduction (Column 1) for each employee by multiplying the Total Earnings by 7.65% (.0765). Round to two decimal places.

3. Determine the federal income tax deduction (Column 2) for each employee by referring to the appropriate line on the tax table either for Single Persons or Married Persons. In the Exemptions column, M-4 means married with four dependents; S-1 means single with one dependent.

4. Calculate the state income tax deduction (Column 3) for each employee by multiplying the federal tax withheld by 19.4% (.194).

5. Add all deductions (Columns 1-4) for each employee; write the result in the Total Deductions column.

6. Subtract Total Deductions from Total Earnings for each employee; write the result in the Net Pay column.

7. Calculate the column totals on the Payroll Register.

8. Verify your calculations. The Total Earnings total minus the Total Deductions total should match the Net Pay total. Also, the totals of Columns 1–4 should equal the Total Deductions total.

TIME CARD

Payroll No. 20   Week Ending June 2
Name Abel, Alice   Exemptions 4
Soc. Sec. No. 055-45-6187   Hourly Rate $9.50

Day	In	Out	Hours
Monday	8	5	8
Tuesday	7	5	9
Wednesday	7	6	10
Thursday	7	6	10
Friday	8	5	8
Saturday	–	–	–

	Rates	Hours	Earnings
Regular	9.50	40	380.00
Overtime	14.25	5	71.25
Totals		45	451.25

TIME CARD

Payroll No. 23   Week Ending June 2
Name Brown, Barbara   Exemptions 2
Soc. Sec. No. 065-38-5178   Hourly Rate $9.65

Day	In	Out	Hours
Monday	8	5	8
Tuesday	8	6	9
Wednesday	7	6	10
Thursday	7	6	10
Friday	8	5	8
Saturday	8	5	8

	Rates	Hours	Earnings
Regular			
Overtime			
Totals			

TIME CARD

Payroll No. 25   Week Ending June 2
Name Cross, Chris   Exemptions 2
Soc. Sec. No. 055-40-8981   Hourly Rate $12.40

Day	In	Out	Hours
Monday	8	5	8
Tuesday	8	3	6
Wednesday	7	6	10
Thursday	7	7	11
Friday	6	9	14
Saturday	8	12	4

	Rates	Hours	Earnings
Regular			
Overtime			
Totals			

TIME CARD

Payroll No. 26   Week Ending June 2
Name Dowe, Don   Exemptions 4
Soc. Sec. No. 055-40-4980   Hourly Rate $14.30

Day	In	Out	Hours
Monday	8	5	8
Tuesday	8	5	8
Wednesday	7	6	10
Thursday	8	5	8
Friday	7	6	10
Saturday	8	3	6

	Rates	Hours	Earnings
Regular			
Overtime			
Totals			

TIME CARD

Payroll No. 48
Name Hopper, Hollis
Soc. Sec. No. 045-40-8190
Week Ending June 2
Exemptions 3
Hourly Rate $15.25

Day	In	Out	Hours
Monday	8	5	8
Tuesday	8	5	8
Wednesday	8	5	8
Thursday	8	5	8
Friday	8	5	8
Saturday	—	—	—

	Hours	Rates	Earnings
Regular			
Overtime			
Totals			

TIME CARD

Payroll No. 60
Name Jenkins, Jettie
Soc. Sec. No. 055-35-6148
Week Ending June 2
Exemptions 2
Hourly Rate $10.55

Day	In	Out	Hours
Monday	8	5	8
Tuesday	8	5	8
Wednesday	8	12	4
Thursday	8	5	8
Friday	8	5	8
Saturday	8	5	8

	Hours	Rates	Earnings
Regular			
Overtime			
Totals			

TIME CARD

Payroll No. 37
Name Ellison, Evelyn
Soc. Sec. No. 065-25-8630
Week Ending June 2
Exemptions 3
Hourly Rate $11.75

Day	In	Out	Hours
Monday	8	3	6
Tuesday	8	5	8
Wednesday	8	5	8
Thursday	6	7	12
Friday	8	5	8
Saturday	8	3	6

	Hours	Rates	Earnings
Regular			
Overtime			
Totals			

TIME CARD

Payroll No. 47
Name Fritz, Fran
Soc. Sec. No. 036-30-7360
Week Ending June 2
Exemptions 1
Hourly Rate $12.60

Day	In	Out	Hours
Monday	8	5	8
Tuesday	8	5	8
Wednesday	8	5	8
Thursday	8	5	8
Friday	8	5	8
Saturday	—	—	—

	Hours	Rates	Earnings
Regular			
Overtime			
Totals			

TIME CARD

Payroll No. 70
Name Markham, Mae
Soc. Sec. No. 060-35-5916
Week Ending June 2
Exemptions 2
Hourly Rate $10.95

Day	In	Out	Hours
Monday	8	5	8
Tuesday	8	3	6
Wednesday	8	5	8
Thursday	8	3	6
Friday	8	3	6
Saturday	8	12	4

	Hours	Rates	Earnings
Regular			
Overtime			
Totals			

TIME CARD

Payroll No. 61
Name Norton, Nick
Soc. Sec. No. 065-30-4678
Week Ending June 2
Exemptions 2
Hourly Rate $11.95

Day	In	Out	Hours
Monday	8	5	8
Tuesday	7	6	10
Wednesday	7	6	10
Thursday	8	5	8
Friday	8	5	8
Saturday	8	12	4

	Hours	Rates	Earnings
Regular			
Overtime			
Totals			

TIME CARD

Payroll No. 55
Name Nelson, Neal
Soc. Sec. No. 065-25-4198
Week Ending June 2
Exemptions 3
Hourly Rate $12.85

Day	In	Out	Hours
Monday	8	5	8
Tuesday	8	5	8
Wednesday	8	5	8
Thursday	8	5	8
Friday	8	5	8
Saturday	8	5	8

	Hours	Rates	Earnings
Regular			
Overtime			
Totals			

TIME CARD

Payroll No. 67
Name Olson, Ossie
Soc. Sec. No. 035-50-9114
Week Ending June 2
Exemptions 1
Hourly Rate $9.85

Day	In	Out	Hours
Monday	8	5	8
Tuesday	8	3	6
Wednesday	8	5	8
Thursday	8	12	4
Friday	8	5	8
Saturday	8	12	4

	Hours	Rates	Earnings
Regular			
Overtime			
Totals			

TIME CARD

Payroll No. 78	Week Ending June 2
Name Paul, Pat	Exemptions 0
Soc. Sec. No. 035-50-0160	Hourly Rate $10.45

Day	In	Out	Hours
Monday	8	3	6
Tuesday	8	5	8
Wednesday	8	3	6
Thursday	8	5	8
Friday	8	3	6
Saturday	8	5	8

	Hours	Rates	Earnings
Regular			
Overtime			
Totals			

TIME CARD

Payroll No. 81	Week Ending June 2
Name Ross, Reese	Exemptions 2
Soc. Sec. No. 045-35-9140	Hourly Rate $12.50

Day	In	Out	Hours
Monday	8	5	8
Tuesday	8	5	8
Wednesday	8	5	8
Thursday	8	5	8
Friday	8	5	8
Saturday	8	5	8

	Hours	Rates	Earnings
Regular			
Overtime			
Totals			

TIME CARD

Payroll No. 79	Week Ending June 2
Name Quick, Kay	Exemptions 1
Soc. Sec. No. 040-40-8880	Hourly Rate $11.80

Day	In	Out	Hours
Monday	8	5	8
Tuesday	8	5	8
Wednesday	8	5	8
Thursday	8	5	8
Friday	8	5	8
Saturday	8	12	4

	Hours	Rates	Earnings
Regular			
Overtime			
Totals			

TIME CARD

Payroll No. 84	Week Ending June 2
Name Schrader, Sandra	Exemptions 1
Soc. Sec. No. 050-25-7350	Hourly Rate $13.10

Day	In	Out	Hours
Monday	8	5	8
Tuesday	8	5	8
Wednesday	–	–	0
Thursday	8	5	8
Friday	8	5	8
Saturday	8	5	8

	Hours	Rates	Earnings
Regular			
Overtime			
Totals			

TIME CARD

Payroll No. 82 Week Ending June 2
Name Scott, Stanley Exemptions 1
Soc. Sec. No. 030-30-8060 Hourly Rate $11.85

Day	In	Out	Hours
Monday	8	5	8
Tuesday	8	5	8
Wednesday	8	5	8
Thursday	8	3	6
Friday	8	3	6
Saturday	8	12	4

	Hours	Rates	Earnings
Regular			
Overtime			
Totals			

TIME CARD

Payroll No. 87 Week Ending June 2
Name Wallace, Walt Exemptions 1
Soc. Sec. No. 065-55-6178 Hourly Rate $13.55

Day	In	Out	Hours
Monday	8	5	8
Tuesday	8	5	8
Wednesday	8	12	4
Thursday	8	5	8
Friday	8	5	8
Saturday	8	5	8

	Hours	Rates	Earnings
Regular			
Overtime			
Totals			

TIME CARD

Payroll No. 85 Week Ending June 2
Name Thomson, Terry Exemptions 1
Soc. Sec. No. 055-25-6214 Hourly Rate $13.45

Day	In	Out	Hours
Monday	8	5	8
Tuesday	8	5	8
Wednesday	8	5	8
Thursday	8	12	4
Friday	8	12	4
Saturday	8	12	4

	Hours	Rates	Earnings
Regular			
Overtime			
Totals			

TIME CARD

Payroll No. 88 Week Ending June 2
Name Zackery, Zack Exemptions 1
Soc. Sec. No. 065-30-4690 Hourly Rate $14.00

Day	In	Out	Hours
Monday	8	5	8
Tuesday	7	6	10
Wednesday	8	5	8
Thursday	7	6	10
Friday	8	5	8
Saturday	7	6	10

	Hours	Rates	Earnings
Regular			
Overtime			
Totals			

SINGLE Persons—WEEKLY Payroll Period

(For Wages Paid in 20--)

If the wages are—		And the number of withholding allowances claimed is—										
At least	But less than	0	1	2	3	4	5	6	7	8	9	10
		The amount of income tax to be withheld is—										
$0	$55	0	0	0	0	0	0	0	0	0	0	0
55	60	1	0	0	0	0	0	0	0	0	0	0
60	65	2	0	0	0	0	0	0	0	0	0	0
65	70	2	0	0	0	0	0	0	0	0	0	0
70	75	3	0	0	0	0	0	0	0	0	0	0
75	80	4	0	0	0	0	0	0	0	0	0	0
80	85	5	0	0	0	0	0	0	0	0	0	0
85	90	5	0	0	0	0	0	0	0	0	0	0
90	95	6	0	0	0	0	0	0	0	0	0	0
95	100	7	0	0	0	0	0	0	0	0	0	0
100	105	8	0	0	0	0	0	0	0	0	0	0
105	110	8	0	0	0	0	0	0	0	0	0	0
110	115	9	1	0	0	0	0	0	0	0	0	0
115	120	10	2	0	0	0	0	0	0	0	0	0
120	125	11	3	0	0	0	0	0	0	0	0	0
125	130	11	3	0	0	0	0	0	0	0	0	0
130	135	12	4	0	0	0	0	0	0	0	0	0
135	140	13	5	0	0	0	0	0	0	0	0	0
140	145	14	6	0	0	0	0	0	0	0	0	0
145	150	14	6	0	0	0	0	0	0	0	0	0
150	155	15	7	0	0	0	0	0	0	0	0	0
155	160	16	8	0	0	0	0	0	0	0	0	0
160	165	17	9	1	0	0	0	0	0	0	0	0
165	170	17	9	1	0	0	0	0	0	0	0	0
170	175	18	10	2	0	0	0	0	0	0	0	0
175	180	19	11	3	0	0	0	0	0	0	0	0
180	185	20	12	4	0	0	0	0	0	0	0	0
185	190	20	12	4	0	0	0	0	0	0	0	0
190	195	21	13	5	0	0	0	0	0	0	0	0
195	200	22	14	6	0	0	0	0	0	0	0	0
200	210	23	15	7	0	0	0	0	0	0	0	0
210	220	25	17	8	0	0	0	0	0	0	0	0
220	230	26	18	10	2	0	0	0	0	0	0	0
230	240	28	20	11	3	0	0	0	0	0	0	0
240	250	29	21	13	5	0	0	0	0	0	0	0
250	260	31	23	14	6	0	0	0	0	0	0	0
260	270	32	24	16	8	0	0	0	0	0	0	0
270	280	34	26	17	9	1	0	0	0	0	0	0
280	290	35	27	19	11	3	0	0	0	0	0	0
290	300	37	29	20	12	4	0	0	0	0	0	0
300	310	38	30	22	14	6	0	0	0	0	0	0
310	320	40	32	23	15	7	0	0	0	0	0	0
320	330	41	33	25	17	9	1	0	0	0	0	0
330	340	43	35	26	18	10	2	0	0	0	0	0
340	350	44	36	28	20	12	4	0	0	0	0	0
350	360	46	38	29	21	13	5	0	0	0	0	0
360	370	47	39	31	23	15	7	0	0	0	0	0
370	380	49	41	32	24	16	8	0	0	0	0	0
380	390	50	42	34	26	18	10	2	0	0	0	0
390	400	52	44	35	27	19	11	3	0	0	0	0
400	410	53	45	37	29	21	13	5	0	0	0	0
410	420	55	47	38	30	22	14	6	0	0	0	0
420	430	56	48	40	32	24	16	8	0	0	0	0
430	440	58	50	41	33	25	17	9	1	0	0	0
440	450	59	51	43	35	27	19	11	3	0	0	0
450	460	61	53	44	36	28	20	12	4	0	0	0
460	470	62	54	46	38	30	22	14	6	0	0	0
470	480	64	56	47	39	31	23	15	7	0	0	0
480	490	65	57	49	41	33	25	17	9	0	0	0
490	500	67	59	50	42	34	26	18	10	2	0	0
500	510	68	60	52	44	36	28	20	12	3	0	0
510	520	70	62	53	45	37	29	21	13	5	0	0
520	530	71	63	55	47	39	31	23	15	6	0	0
530	540	73	65	56	48	40	32	24	16	8	0	0
540	550	75	66	58	50	42	34	26	18	9	1	0
550	560	78	68	59	51	43	35	27	19	11	3	0
560	570	81	69	61	53	45	37	29	21	12	4	0
570	580	84	71	62	54	46	38	30	22	14	6	0
580	590	87	72	64	56	48	40	32	24	15	7	0
590	600	89	74	65	57	49	41	33	25	17	9	1

SINGLE Persons—WEEKLY Payroll Period
(For Wages Paid in 20--)

If the wages are—		And the number of withholding allowances claimed is—										
At least	But less than	0	1	2	3	4	5	6	7	8	9	10
		The amount of income tax to be withheld is—										
$600	$610	92	77	67	59	51	43	35	27	18	10	2
610	620	95	80	68	60	52	44	36	28	20	12	4
620	630	98	83	70	62	54	46	38	30	21	13	5
630	640	101	85	71	63	55	47	39	31	23	15	7
640	650	103	88	73	65	57	49	41	33	24	16	8
650	660	106	91	76	66	58	50	42	34	26	18	10
660	670	109	94	79	68	60	52	44	36	27	19	11
670	680	112	97	82	69	61	53	45	37	29	21	13
680	690	115	99	84	71	63	55	47	39	30	22	14
690	700	117	102	87	72	64	56	48	40	32	24	16
700	710	120	105	90	75	66	58	50	42	33	25	17
710	720	123	108	93	78	67	59	51	43	35	27	19
720	730	126	111	96	81	69	61	53	45	36	28	20
730	740	129	113	98	83	70	62	54	46	38	30	22
740	750	131	116	101	86	72	64	56	48	39	31	23
750	760	134	119	104	89	74	65	57	49	41	33	25
760	770	137	122	107	92	77	67	59	51	42	34	26
770	780	140	125	110	95	79	68	60	52	44	36	28
780	790	143	127	112	97	82	70	62	54	45	37	29
790	800	145	130	115	100	85	71	63	55	47	39	31
800	810	148	133	118	103	88	73	65	57	48	40	32
810	820	151	136	121	106	91	76	66	58	50	42	34
820	830	154	139	124	109	93	78	68	60	51	43	35
830	840	157	141	126	111	96	81	69	61	53	45	37
840	850	159	144	129	114	99	84	71	63	54	46	38
850	860	162	147	132	117	102	87	72	64	56	48	40
860	870	165	150	135	120	105	90	74	66	57	49	41
870	880	168	153	138	123	107	92	77	67	59	51	43
880	890	171	155	140	125	110	95	80	69	60	52	44
890	900	173	158	143	128	113	98	83	70	62	54	46
900	910	176	161	146	131	116	101	86	72	63	55	47
910	920	179	164	149	134	119	104	88	73	65	57	49
920	930	182	167	152	137	121	106	91	76	66	58	50
930	940	185	169	154	139	124	109	94	79	68	60	52
940	950	187	172	157	142	127	112	97	82	69	61	53
950	960	190	175	160	145	130	115	100	85	71	63	55
960	970	193	178	163	148	133	118	102	87	72	64	56
970	980	196	181	166	151	135	120	105	90	75	66	58
980	990	199	183	168	153	138	123	108	93	78	67	59
990	1,000	201	186	171	156	141	126	111	96	81	69	61
1,000	1,010	204	189	174	159	144	129	114	99	84	70	62
1,010	1,020	207	192	177	162	147	132	116	101	86	72	64
1,020	1,030	210	195	180	165	149	134	119	104	89	74	65
1,030	1,040	213	197	182	167	152	137	122	107	92	77	67
1,040	1,050	215	200	185	170	155	140	125	110	95	80	68
1,050	1,060	218	203	188	173	158	143	128	113	98	82	70
1,060	1,070	221	206	191	176	161	146	130	115	100	85	71
1,070	1,080	224	209	194	179	163	148	133	118	103	88	73
1,080	1,090	227	211	196	181	166	151	136	121	106	91	76
1,090	1,100	229	214	199	184	169	154	139	124	109	94	79
1,100	1,110	232	217	202	187	172	157	142	127	112	96	81
1,110	1,120	235	220	205	190	175	160	144	129	114	99	84
1,120	1,130	238	223	208	193	177	162	147	132	117	102	87
1,130	1,140	241	225	210	195	180	165	150	135	120	105	90
1,140	1,150	243	228	213	198	183	168	153	138	123	108	93
1,150	1,160	246	231	216	201	186	171	156	141	126	110	95
1,160	1,170	249	234	219	204	189	174	158	143	128	113	98
1,170	1,180	252	237	222	207	191	176	161	146	131	116	101
1,180	1,190	256	239	224	209	194	179	164	149	134	119	104
1,190	1,200	259	242	227	212	197	182	167	152	137	122	107
1,200	1,210	262	245	230	215	200	185	170	155	140	124	109
1,210	1,220	265	248	233	218	203	188	172	157	142	127	112
1,220	1,230	268	251	236	221	205	190	175	160	145	130	115
1,230	1,240	271	254	238	223	208	193	178	163	148	133	118
1,240	1,250	274	257	241	226	211	196	181	166	151	136	121

MARRIED Persons—WEEKLY Payroll Period

(For Wages Paid in 20--)

If the wages are—		And the number of withholding allowances claimed is—										
At least	But less than	0	1	2	3	4	5	6	7	8	9	10
		The amount of income tax to be withheld is—										
$0	$125	0	0	0	0	0	0	0	0	0	0	0
125	130	1	0	0	0	0	0	0	0	0	0	0
130	135	1	0	0	0	0	0	0	0	0	0	0
135	140	2	0	0	0	0	0	0	0	0	0	0
140	145	3	0	0	0	0	0	0	0	0	0	0
145	150	4	0	0	0	0	0	0	0	0	0	0
150	155	4	0	0	0	0	0	0	0	0	0	0
155	160	5	0	0	0	0	0	0	0	0	0	0
160	165	6	0	0	0	0	0	0	0	0	0	0
165	170	7	0	0	0	0	0	0	0	0	0	0
170	175	7	0	0	0	0	0	0	0	0	0	0
175	180	8	0	0	0	0	0	0	0	0	0	0
180	185	9	1	0	0	0	0	0	0	0	0	0
185	190	10	1	0	0	0	0	0	0	0	0	0
190	195	10	2	0	0	0	0	0	0	0	0	0
195	200	11	3	0	0	0	0	0	0	0	0	0
200	210	12	4	0	0	0	0	0	0	0	0	0
210	220	14	6	0	0	0	0	0	0	0	0	0
220	230	15	7	0	0	0	0	0	0	0	0	0
230	240	17	9	0	0	0	0	0	0	0	0	0
240	250	18	10	2	0	0	0	0	0	0	0	0
250	260	20	12	3	0	0	0	0	0	0	0	0
260	270	21	13	5	0	0	0	0	0	0	0	0
270	280	23	15	6	0	0	0	0	0	0	0	0
280	290	24	16	8	0	0	0	0	0	0	0	0
290	300	26	18	9	1	0	0	0	0	0	0	0
300	310	27	19	11	3	0	0	0	0	0	0	0
310	320	29	21	12	4	0	0	0	0	0	0	0
320	330	30	22	14	6	0	0	0	0	0	0	0
330	340	32	24	15	7	0	0	0	0	0	0	0
340	350	33	25	17	9	1	0	0	0	0	0	0
350	360	35	27	18	10	2	0	0	0	0	0	0
360	370	36	28	20	12	4	0	0	0	0	0	0
370	380	38	30	21	13	5	0	0	0	0	0	0
380	390	39	31	23	15	7	0	0	0	0	0	0
390	400	41	33	24	16	8	0	0	0	0	0	0
400	410	42	34	26	18	10	2	0	0	0	0	0
410	420	44	36	27	19	11	3	0	0	0	0	0
420	430	45	37	29	21	13	5	0	0	0	0	0
430	440	47	39	30	22	14	6	0	0	0	0	0
440	450	48	40	32	24	16	8	0	0	0	0	0
450	460	50	42	33	25	17	9	1	0	0	0	0
460	470	51	43	35	27	19	11	3	0	0	0	0
470	480	53	45	36	28	20	12	4	0	0	0	0
480	490	54	46	38	30	22	14	6	0	0	0	0
490	500	56	48	39	31	23	15	7	0	0	0	0
500	510	57	49	41	33	25	17	9	1	0	0	0
510	520	59	51	42	34	26	18	10	2	0	0	0
520	530	60	52	44	36	28	20	12	4	0	0	0
530	540	62	54	45	37	29	21	13	5	0	0	0
540	550	63	55	47	39	31	23	15	7	0	0	0
550	560	65	57	48	40	32	24	16	8	0	0	0
560	570	66	58	50	42	34	26	18	10	2	0	0
570	580	68	60	51	43	35	27	19	11	3	0	0
580	590	69	61	53	45	37	29	21	13	5	0	0
590	600	71	63	54	46	38	30	22	14	6	0	0
600	610	72	64	56	48	40	32	24	16	8	0	0
610	620	74	66	57	49	41	33	25	17	9	1	0
620	630	75	67	59	51	43	35	27	19	11	2	0
630	640	77	69	60	52	44	36	28	20	12	4	0
640	650	78	70	62	54	46	38	30	22	14	5	0
650	660	80	72	63	55	47	39	31	23	15	7	0
660	670	81	73	65	57	49	41	33	25	17	8	0
670	680	83	75	66	58	50	42	34	26	18	10	2
680	690	84	76	68	60	52	44	36	28	20	11	3
690	700	86	78	69	61	53	45	37	29	21	13	5
700	710	87	79	71	63	55	47	39	31	23	14	6
710	720	89	81	72	64	56	48	40	32	24	16	8
720	730	90	82	74	66	58	50	42	34	26	17	9
730	740	92	84	75	67	59	51	43	35	27	19	11

MARRIED Persons—WEEKLY Payroll Period
(For Wages Paid in 20--)

If the wages are—		And the number of withholding allowances claimed is—										
At least	But less than	0	1	2	3	4	5	6	7	8	9	10
		The amount of income tax to be withheld is—										
$740	$750	93	85	77	69	61	53	45	37	29	20	12
750	760	95	87	78	70	62	54	46	38	30	22	14
760	770	96	88	80	72	64	56	48	40	32	23	15
770	780	98	90	81	73	65	57	49	41	33	25	17
780	790	99	91	83	75	67	59	51	43	35	26	18
790	800	101	93	84	76	68	60	52	44	36	28	20
800	810	102	94	86	78	70	62	54	46	38	29	21
810	820	104	96	87	79	71	63	55	47	39	31	23
820	830	105	97	89	81	73	65	57	49	41	32	24
830	840	107	99	90	82	74	66	58	50	42	34	26
840	850	108	100	92	84	76	68	60	52	44	35	27
850	860	110	102	93	85	77	69	61	53	45	37	29
860	870	111	103	95	87	79	71	63	55	47	38	30
870	880	113	105	96	88	80	72	64	56	48	40	32
880	890	114	106	98	90	82	74	66	58	50	41	33
890	900	116	108	99	91	83	75	67	59	51	43	35
900	910	117	109	101	93	85	77	69	61	53	44	36
910	920	119	111	102	94	86	78	70	62	54	46	38
920	930	120	112	104	96	88	80	72	64	56	47	39
930	940	122	114	105	97	89	81	73	65	57	49	41
940	950	125	115	107	99	91	83	75	67	59	50	42
950	960	128	117	108	100	92	84	76	68	60	52	44
960	970	131	118	110	102	94	86	78	70	62	53	45
970	980	133	120	111	103	95	87	79	71	63	55	47
980	990	136	121	113	105	97	89	81	73	65	56	48
990	1,000	139	124	114	106	98	90	82	74	66	58	50
1,000	1,010	142	127	116	108	100	92	84	76	68	59	51
1,010	1,020	145	130	117	109	101	93	85	77	69	61	53
1,020	1,030	147	132	119	111	103	95	87	79	71	62	54
1,030	1,040	150	135	120	112	104	96	88	80	72	64	56
1,040	1,050	153	138	123	114	106	98	90	82	74	65	57
1,050	1,060	156	141	126	115	107	99	91	83	75	67	59
1,060	1,070	159	144	128	117	109	101	93	85	77	68	60
1,070	1,080	161	146	131	118	110	102	94	86	78	70	62
1,080	1,090	164	149	134	120	112	104	96	88	80	71	63
1,090	1,100	167	152	137	122	113	105	97	89	81	73	65
1,100	1,110	170	155	140	125	115	107	99	91	83	74	66
1,110	1,120	173	158	142	127	116	108	100	92	84	76	68
1,120	1,130	175	160	145	130	118	110	102	94	86	77	69
1,130	1,140	178	163	148	133	119	111	103	95	87	79	71
1,140	1,150	181	166	151	136	121	113	105	97	89	80	72
1,150	1,160	184	169	154	139	123	114	106	98	90	82	74
1,160	1,170	187	172	156	141	126	116	108	100	92	83	75
1,170	1,180	189	174	159	144	129	117	109	101	93	85	77
1,180	1,190	192	177	162	147	132	119	111	103	95	86	78
1,190	1,200	195	180	165	150	135	120	112	104	96	88	80
1,200	1,210	198	183	168	153	137	122	114	106	98	89	81
1,210	1,220	201	186	170	155	140	125	115	107	99	91	83
1,220	1,230	203	188	173	158	143	128	117	109	101	92	84
1,230	1,240	206	191	176	161	146	131	118	110	102	94	86
1,240	1,250	209	194	179	164	149	134	120	112	104	95	87
1,250	1,260	212	197	182	167	151	136	121	113	105	97	89
1,260	1,270	215	200	184	169	154	139	124	115	107	98	90
1,270	1,280	217	202	187	172	157	142	127	116	108	100	92
1,280	1,290	220	205	190	175	160	145	130	118	110	101	93
1,290	1,300	223	208	193	178	163	148	133	119	111	103	95
1,300	1,310	226	211	196	181	165	150	135	121	113	104	96
1,310	1,320	229	214	198	183	168	153	138	123	114	106	98
1,320	1,330	231	216	201	186	171	156	141	126	116	107	99
1,330	1,340	234	219	204	189	174	159	144	129	117	109	101
1,340	1,350	237	222	207	192	177	162	147	131	119	110	102
1,350	1,360	240	225	210	195	179	164	149	134	120	112	104
1,360	1,370	243	228	212	197	182	167	152	137	122	113	105
1,370	1,380	245	230	215	200	185	170	155	140	125	115	107
1,380	1,390	248	233	218	203	188	173	158	143	128	116	108

Crown Distributing Co. Payroll Register

Week Ended: June 2 **Date of Payment:** June 2

Name	Exemptions	Total Earnings	1 FICA Tax	2 Federal Tax	3 State Tax	4 Insurance	Total Deductions	Net Pay
Abel, Alice	M-4	$ 451.25	$ 34.52	$ 17.00	$ 3.30	$ 60.15	$ 114.97	$ 336.28
Brown, Barbara	S-2					60.15		
Cross, Chris	M-2					60.15		
Dowe, Don	M-4					60.15		
Ellison, Evelyn	M-3					60.15		
Fritz, Fran	S-1					35.50		
Hopper, Hollis	M-3					60.15		
Jenkins, Jettie	M-2					60.15		
Markham, Mae	M-2					60.15		
Nelson, Neal	M-3					60.15		
Norton, Nick	M-2					60.15		
Olson, Ossie	S-1					35.50		
Paul, Pat	S-0					35.50		
Quick, Kay	S-1					35.50		
Ross, Reese	M-2					60.15		
Schrader, Sandra	S-1					35.50		
Scott, Stanley	S-1					35.50		
Thomson, Terry	S-1					35.50		
Wallace, Walt	S-1					35.50		
Zackery, Zack	S-1					35.50		
Totals		$	$	$	$	$	$	$

175

Application 4-6

Determine Salary Plus Commission Payroll

OBJECTIVES

Upon completion of this application, you will be able to:

1. Calculate earnings based on commission.

2. Complete individual earnings records.

3. Transfer data and complete a payroll record.

4. Determine gross earnings.

5. Calculate FICA and state income tax withholdings.

6. Read tax charts to determine federal income tax withholdings.

7. Calculate total deductions and net earnings.

INSTRUCTIONS

Salary plus commission-based employees are paid a standard salary plus a commission on sales instead of an hourly, weekly, or monthly wage. Commissions are calculated by multiplying the total value of the products sold by the commission rate. The total commission earned is then added to the base salary.

Calculate each employee's commission earnings for the month as follows (the first employee's Monthly Commission Record has been completed for you):

1. Transfer from the Commission Calculation Table the value of each product sold into the Value column.

2. For each product, multiply the Value by the Units Sold; write the result in the Total Sale column.

3. Transfer from the Commission Calculation Table the commission rate for each product into the Commission Rate column.

4. For each product, multiply the Total Sale by the Commission Rate; write the result in the Commission Earned column.

5. Calculate the totals of the Units Sold, Total Sale, and Commission Earned columns.

6. Complete the remaining nine Montly Commission Records by following the procedures given in Steps 1-5.

After you have completed all employee commission records, complete the Payroll Record as follows:

1. Transfer the commission earnings from each employee record to the Commission column of the Payroll Record.

2. Add the Commission to the Salary; write the result in the Gross Earnings column.

3. Calculate the FICA tax deduction for each employee by multiplying the Gross Earnings by 7.65% (.0765). Round to two decimal places.

4. Determine the federal income tax deduction for each employee by looking up the Gross Earnings figure in the appropriate tax table. In the Dependents column, M-3 means married with three dependents; S-2 means single with two dependents.

5. Calculate the state income tax deduction for each employee by multiplying the federal tax withheld by 21.23% (.2123).

6. Refer to the Deductions chart for Dues, Charities, Credit Union, and Employee Purchases to be deducted. Note that the number of deductions varies for each employee. Transfer each employee's deductions to the appropriate column and line on the Payroll Record.

7. For each employee, subtract the deductions from the Gross Earnings; write the result in the Net Earnings column.

8. Calculate the column totals on the Payroll Record.

9. Verify your calculations. The Gross Earnings total minus the total of each deduction column should match the Net Earnings total. The Salary total plus the Commission total should equal the Gross Earnings total.

COMMISSION CALCULATION TABLE

Product	Value	Commission Rate
Desktop Computer	$719.00	5%
Laptop Computer	1,243.00	6.5%
Monitor CRT	110.00	2.25%
Monitor Flat Panel 17"	425.00	2.75%
Ink Jet Printer	349.00	3.25%
Color Laser Printer	388.00	4%
Multifunction (4 in 1)	498.00	6.25%
Scanner	179.00	7%
Fax	149.95	3.5%

MONTHLY COMMISSION RECORD for _Ammons, Louise B._
Last Name   First Name   Initial

Month of _February_

Product	Units Sold	Value	Total Sale	Commission Rate	Commission Earned
Desktop Computer	5	$ 719.00	$ 3,595.00	5%	$ 179.75
Monitor CRT	7	110.00	770.00	2.25%	17.33
Fax	10	149.95	1,499.50	3.5%	52.48
Ink Jet Printer	2	349.49	698.98	3.25%	22.69
Totals	24		$ 6,563.50		$ 272.25

MONTHLY COMMISSION RECORD for

Clounte, Jose P.
Last Name / First Name / Initial
Month of February

Product	Units Sold	Value	Total Sale	Commission Rate	Commission Earned
Scanner	4	$	$		$
Fax	9				
Monitor Flat Panel 17"	3				
Totals			$		$

MONTHLY COMMISSION RECORD for

Iverson, Douglas L.
Last Name / First Name / Initial
Month of February

Product	Units Sold	Value	Total Sale	Commission Rate	Commission Earned
Laptop Computer	4	$	$		$
Monitor CRT	2				
Color Laser Printer	5				
Scanner	2				
Totals			$		$

MONTHLY COMMISSION RECORD for

Doverspike, Bob R.
Last Name / First Name / Initial
Month of February

Product	Units Sold	Value	Total Sale	Commission Rate	Commission Earned
Desktop Computer	2	$	$		$
Monitor Flat Panel 17"	2				
Ink Jet Printer	1				
Multifunction	1				
Totals			$		$

MONTHLY COMMISSION RECORD for

Leeson, Faye W.
Last Name / First Name / Initial
Month of February

Product	Units Sold	Value	Total Sale	Commission Rate	Commission Earned
Multifunction	4	$	$		$
Fax	5				
Totals			$		$

MONTHLY COMMISSION RECORD for

Last Name: Smither First Name: Connie Initial: R.
Month of: February

Product	Units Sold	Value	Total Sale	Commission Rate	Commission Earned
Laptop Computer	4	$	$		$
Ink Jet Printer	6				
Color Laser Printer	2				
Fax	2				
Totals			$		$

MONTHLY COMMISSION RECORD for

Last Name: Youchoff First Name: Helena Initial: C.
Month of: February

Product	Units Sold	Value	Total Sale	Commission Rate	Commission Earned
Ink Jet Printer	9	$	$		$
Scanner	6				
Fax	3				
Totals			$		$

MONTHLY COMMISSION RECORD for

Last Name: McXanders First Name: Annique Initial: A.
Month of: February

Product	Units Sold	Value	Total Sale	Commission Rate	Commission Earned
Desktop Computer	7	$	$		$
Monitor CRJ	7				
Ink Jet Printer	4				
Color Laser Printer	2				
Multifunction	1				
Totals			$		$

MONTHLY COMMISSION RECORD for

Last Name: Peebles First Name: Samantha Initial: J.
Month of: February

Product	Units Sold	Value	Total Sale	Commission Rate	Commission Earned
Desktop Computer	3	$	$		$
Ink Jet Printer	6				
Scanner	7				
Totals			$		$

MONTHLY COMMISSION RECORD for

Jane, Nancy X.
Last Name   First Name   Initial

Month of _February_

Product	Units Sold	Value	Total Sale	Commission Rate	Commission Earned
Desktop Computer	8	$	$		$
Monitor CRT	8				
Ink Jet Printer	2				
Color Laser Printer	2				
Multifunction	5				
Scanner	1				
Totals			$		$

CHOICE COMPUTER SYSTEMS, INCORPORATED
PAYROLL RECORD for the month of _February_

Employee (Last Name, Initials)	Salary	Commission	Gross Earnings	FICA Tax	Dependents	Federal Tax	State Tax	Dues	Charities	Credit Union	Employee Purchases	Net Earnings
Ammons, L. B.	$ 1,700.00	$	$	$	S-1	$	$	$	$	$	$	$
Clonts, J. P.	1,875.00				S-0							
Doverspike, B. R.	1,850.00				M-1							
Iverson, D. H.	2,025.00				S-1							
Leeson, F. W.	1,750.00				M-5							
McXanders, A. A.	2,000.00				M-4							
Peeples, S. J.	1,975.00				M-3							
Smither, C. R.	2,275.00				S-2							
Youchoff, H. C.	1,825.00				S-3							
Zane, N. X.	2,750.00				M-2							
Totals	$	$	$	$		$	$	$	$	$	$	$

Deductions

DUES

Employee Name	Amount Deducted
Ammons, L.B.	2.25
Clounts, J.P.	2.25
Doverspike, B.R.	2.25
Leeson, F.W.	2.25
McXanders, A.A.	2.25
Peebles, S.G.	2.25
Smither, C.R.	2.25
Youchoff, H.C.	2.25

CHARITIES

Employee Name	Amount Deducted
Clounts, J.P.	5.00
Doverspike, B.R.	8.00
Leeson, F.W.	6.00
Peebles, S.G.	2.00
Smither, C.R.	3.00

CREDIT UNION

Employee Name	Amount Deducted
Ammons, L.B.	25.00
Clounts, J.P.	10.00
Doverspike, B.R.	10.00
Leeson, F.W.	15.00
McXanders, A.A.	2.00
Youchoff, H.C.	6.00

EMPLOYEE PURCHASES

Employee Name	Amount Deducted
Ammons, L.B.	35.00
Leeson, F.W.	41.00
Peebles, S.G.	56.00
Smither, C.R.	39.00
Youchoff, H.C.	45.00

SINGLE Persons—MONTHLY Payroll Period

(For Wages Paid Through December 20--)

If the wages are—		And the number of withholding allowances claimed is—										
At least	But less than	0	1	2	3	4	5	6	7	8	9	10
		The amount of income tax to be withheld is—										
$0	$230	$0	$0	$0	$0	$0	$0	$0	$0	$0	$0	$0
230	240	1	0	0	0	0	0	0	0	0	0	0
240	250	2	0	0	0	0	0	0	0	0	0	0
250	260	3	0	0	0	0	0	0	0	0	0	0
260	270	4	0	0	0	0	0	0	0	0	0	0
270	280	5	0	0	0	0	0	0	0	0	0	0
280	290	6	0	0	0	0	0	0	0	0	0	0
290	300	7	0	0	0	0	0	0	0	0	0	0
300	320	9	0	0	0	0	0	0	0	0	0	0
320	340	11	0	0	0	0	0	0	0	0	0	0
340	360	13	0	0	0	0	0	0	0	0	0	0
360	380	15	0	0	0	0	0	0	0	0	0	0
380	400	17	0	0	0	0	0	0	0	0	0	0
400	420	19	0	0	0	0	0	0	0	0	0	0
420	440	21	0	0	0	0	0	0	0	0	0	0
440	460	23	0	0	0	0	0	0	0	0	0	0
460	480	25	0	0	0	0	0	0	0	0	0	0
480	500	27	1	0	0	0	0	0	0	0	0	0
500	520	29	3	0	0	0	0	0	0	0	0	0
520	540	31	5	0	0	0	0	0	0	0	0	0
540	560	33	7	0	0	0	0	0	0	0	0	0
560	580	35	9	0	0	0	0	0	0	0	0	0
580	600	37	11	0	0	0	0	0	0	0	0	0
600	640	40	14	0	0	0	0	0	0	0	0	0
640	680	44	18	0	0	0	0	0	0	0	0	0
680	720	48	22	0	0	0	0	0	0	0	0	0
720	760	52	26	0	0	0	0	0	0	0	0	0
760	800	56	30	4	0	0	0	0	0	0	0	0
800	840	61	34	8	0	0	0	0	0	0	0	0
840	880	67	38	12	0	0	0	0	0	0	0	0
880	920	73	42	16	0	0	0	0	0	0	0	0
920	960	79	46	20	0	0	0	0	0	0	0	0
960	1,000	85	50	24	0	0	0	0	0	0	0	0
1,000	1,040	91	54	28	2	0	0	0	0	0	0	0
1,040	1,080	97	58	32	6	0	0	0	0	0	0	0
1,080	1,120	103	64	36	10	0	0	0	0	0	0	0
1,120	1,160	109	70	40	14	0	0	0	0	0	0	0
1,160	1,200	115	76	44	18	0	0	0	0	0	0	0
1,200	1,240	121	82	48	22	0	0	0	0	0	0	0
1,240	1,280	127	88	52	26	1	0	0	0	0	0	0
1,280	1,320	133	94	56	30	5	0	0	0	0	0	0
1,320	1,360	139	100	61	34	9	0	0	0	0	0	0
1,360	1,400	145	106	67	38	13	0	0	0	0	0	0
1,400	1,440	151	112	73	42	17	0	0	0	0	0	0
1,440	1,480	157	118	79	46	21	0	0	0	0	0	0
1,480	1,520	163	124	85	50	25	0	0	0	0	0	0
1,520	1,560	169	130	91	54	29	3	0	0	0	0	0
1,560	1,600	175	136	97	58	33	7	0	0	0	0	0
1,600	1,640	181	142	103	64	37	11	0	0	0	0	0
1,640	1,680	187	148	109	70	41	15	0	0	0	0	0
1,680	1,720	193	154	115	76	45	19	0	0	0	0	0
1,720	1,760	199	160	121	82	49	23	0	0	0	0	0
1,760	1,800	205	166	127	88	53	27	1	0	0	0	0
1,800	1,840	211	172	133	94	57	31	5	0	0	0	0
1,840	1,880	217	178	139	100	62	35	9	0	0	0	0
1,880	1,920	223	184	145	106	68	39	13	0	0	0	0
1,920	1,960	229	190	151	112	74	43	17	0	0	0	0
1,960	2,000	235	196	157	118	80	47	21	0	0	0	0
2,000	2,040	241	202	163	124	86	51	25	0	0	0	0
2,040	2,080	247	208	169	130	92	55	29	3	0	0	0
2,080	2,120	253	214	175	136	98	59	33	7	0	0	0
2,120	2,160	259	220	181	142	104	65	37	11	0	0	0
2,160	2,200	265	226	187	148	110	71	41	15	0	0	0
2,200	2,240	271	232	193	154	116	77	45	19	0	0	0
2,240	2,280	277	238	199	160	122	83	49	23	0	0	0
2,280	2,320	283	244	205	166	128	89	53	27	1	0	0
2,320	2,360	289	250	211	172	134	95	57	31	5	0	0
2,360	2,400	295	256	217	178	140	101	62	35	9	0	0
2,400	2,440	301	262	223	184	146	107	68	39	13	0	0
2,440	2,480	307	268	229	190	152	113	74	43	17	0	0

SINGLE Persons—MONTHLY Payroll Period

(For Wages Paid Through December 20--)

If the wages are—		And the number of withholding allowances claimed is—										
At least	But less than	0	1	2	3	4	5	6	7	8	9	10
		The amount of income tax to be withheld is—										
$2,480	$2,520	$313	$274	$235	$196	$158	$119	$80	$47	$21	$0	$0
2,520	2,560	319	280	241	202	164	125	86	51	25	0	0
2,560	2,600	326	286	247	208	170	131	92	55	29	3	0
2,600	2,640	336	292	253	214	176	137	98	59	33	7	0
2,640	2,680	346	298	259	220	182	143	104	65	37	11	0
2,680	2,720	356	304	265	226	188	149	110	71	41	15	0
2,720	2,760	366	310	271	232	194	155	116	77	45	19	0
2,760	2,800	376	316	277	238	200	161	122	83	49	23	0
2,800	2,840	386	322	283	244	206	167	128	89	53	27	2
2,840	2,880	396	331	289	250	212	173	134	95	57	31	6
2,880	2,920	406	341	295	256	218	179	140	101	63	35	10
2,920	2,960	416	351	301	262	224	185	146	107	69	39	14
2,960	3,000	426	361	307	268	230	191	152	113	75	43	18
3,000	3,040	436	371	313	274	236	197	158	119	81	47	22
3,040	3,080	446	381	319	280	242	203	164	125	87	51	26
3,080	3,120	456	391	327	286	248	209	170	131	93	55	30
3,120	3,160	466	401	337	292	254	215	176	137	99	60	34
3,160	3,200	476	411	347	298	260	221	182	143	105	66	38
3,200	3,240	486	421	357	304	266	227	188	149	111	72	42
3,240	3,280	496	431	367	310	272	233	194	155	117	78	46
3,280	3,320	506	441	377	316	278	239	200	161	123	84	50
3,320	3,360	516	451	387	322	284	245	206	167	129	90	54
3,360	3,400	526	461	397	332	290	251	212	173	135	96	58
3,400	3,440	536	471	407	342	296	257	218	179	141	102	63
3,440	3,480	546	481	417	352	302	263	224	185	147	108	69
3,480	3,520	556	491	427	362	308	269	230	191	153	114	75
3,520	3,560	566	501	437	372	314	275	236	197	159	120	81
3,560	3,600	576	511	447	382	320	281	242	203	165	126	87
3,600	3,640	586	521	457	392	328	287	248	209	171	132	93
3,640	3,680	596	531	467	402	338	293	254	215	177	138	99
3,680	3,720	606	541	477	412	348	299	260	221	183	144	105
3,720	3,760	616	551	487	422	358	305	266	227	189	150	111
3,760	3,800	626	561	497	432	368	311	272	233	195	156	117
3,800	3,840	636	571	507	442	378	317	278	239	201	162	123
3,840	3,880	646	581	517	452	388	323	284	245	207	168	129
3,880	3,920	656	591	527	462	398	333	290	251	213	174	135
3,920	3,960	666	601	537	472	408	343	296	257	219	180	141
3,960	4,000	676	611	547	482	418	353	302	263	225	186	147
4,000	4,040	686	621	557	492	428	363	308	269	231	192	153
4,040	4,080	696	631	567	502	438	373	314	275	237	198	159
4,080	4,120	706	641	577	512	448	383	320	281	243	204	165
4,120	4,160	716	651	587	522	458	393	328	287	249	210	171
4,160	4,200	726	661	597	532	468	403	338	293	255	216	177
4,200	4,240	736	671	607	542	478	413	348	299	261	222	183
4,240	4,280	746	681	617	552	488	423	358	305	267	228	189
4,280	4,320	756	691	627	562	498	433	368	311	273	234	195
4,320	4,360	766	701	637	572	508	443	378	317	279	240	201
4,360	4,400	776	711	647	582	518	453	388	324	285	246	207
4,400	4,440	786	721	657	592	528	463	398	334	291	252	213
4,440	4,480	796	731	667	602	538	473	408	344	297	258	219
4,480	4,520	806	741	677	612	548	483	418	354	303	264	225
4,520	4,560	816	751	687	622	558	493	428	364	309	270	231
4,560	4,600	826	761	697	632	568	503	438	374	315	276	237
4,600	4,640	836	771	707	642	578	513	448	384	321	282	243
4,640	4,680	846	781	717	652	588	523	458	394	329	288	249
4,680	4,720	856	791	727	662	598	533	468	404	339	294	255
4,720	4,760	866	801	737	672	608	543	478	414	349	300	261
4,760	4,800	876	811	747	682	618	553	488	424	359	306	267
4,800	4,840	886	821	757	692	628	563	498	434	369	312	273
4,840	4,880	896	831	767	702	638	573	508	444	379	318	279
4,880	4,920	906	841	777	712	648	583	518	454	389	325	285
4,920	4,960	916	851	787	722	658	593	528	464	399	335	291
4,960	5,000	926	861	797	732	668	603	538	474	409	345	297
5,000	5,040	936	871	807	742	678	613	548	484	419	355	303
5,040	5,080	946	881	817	752	688	623	558	494	429	365	309

$5,080 and over   Use Table 4(a) for a **SINGLE person** on page 3. Also see the instructions on page 2.

MARRIED Persons—MONTHLY Payroll Period

(For Wages Paid Through December 20--)

If the wages are–		And the number of withholding allowances claimed is—										
At least	But less than	0	1	2	3	4	5	6	7	8	9	10
		The amount of income tax to be withheld is—										
$0	$540	$0	$0	$0	$0	$0	$0	$0	$0	$0	$0	$0
540	560	0	0	0	0	0	0	0	0	0	0	0
560	580	0	0	0	0	0	0	0	0	0	0	0
580	600	0	0	0	0	0	0	0	0	0	0	0
600	640	0	0	0	0	0	0	0	0	0	0	0
640	680	0	0	0	0	0	0	0	0	0	0	0
680	720	3	0	0	0	0	0	0	0	0	0	0
720	760	7	0	0	0	0	0	0	0	0	0	0
760	800	11	0	0	0	0	0	0	0	0	0	0
800	840	15	0	0	0	0	0	0	0	0	0	0
840	880	19	0	0	0	0	0	0	0	0	0	0
880	920	23	0	0	0	0	0	0	0	0	0	0
920	960	27	2	0	0	0	0	0	0	0	0	0
960	1,000	31	6	0	0	0	0	0	0	0	0	0
1,000	1,040	35	10	0	0	0	0	0	0	0	0	0
1,040	1,080	39	14	0	0	0	0	0	0	0	0	0
1,080	1,120	43	18	0	0	0	0	0	0	0	0	0
1,120	1,160	47	22	0	0	0	0	0	0	0	0	0
1,160	1,200	51	26	0	0	0	0	0	0	0	0	0
1,200	1,240	55	30	4	0	0	0	0	0	0	0	0
1,240	1,280	59	34	8	0	0	0	0	0	0	0	0
1,280	1,320	63	38	12	0	0	0	0	0	0	0	0
1,320	1,360	67	42	16	0	0	0	0	0	0	0	0
1,360	1,400	71	46	20	0	0	0	0	0	0	0	0
1,400	1,440	75	50	24	0	0	0	0	0	0	0	0
1,440	1,480	79	54	28	2	0	0	0	0	0	0	0
1,480	1,520	83	58	32	6	0	0	0	0	0	0	0
1,520	1,560	87	62	36	10	0	0	0	0	0	0	0
1,560	1,600	91	66	40	14	0	0	0	0	0	0	0
1,600	1,640	95	70	44	18	0	0	0	0	0	0	0
1,640	1,680	99	74	48	22	0	0	0	0	0	0	0
1,680	1,720	103	78	52	26	0	0	0	0	0	0	0
1,720	1,760	107	82	56	30	4	0	0	0	0	0	0
1,760	1,800	111	86	60	34	8	0	0	0	0	0	0
1,800	1,840	115	90	64	38	12	0	0	0	0	0	0
1,840	1,880	119	94	68	42	16	0	0	0	0	0	0
1,880	1,920	125	98	72	46	20	0	0	0	0	0	0
1,920	1,960	131	102	76	50	24	0	0	0	0	0	0
1,960	2,000	137	106	80	54	28	2	0	0	0	0	0
2,000	2,040	143	110	84	58	32	6	0	0	0	0	0
2,040	2,080	149	114	88	62	36	10	0	0	0	0	0
2,080	2,120	155	118	92	66	40	14	0	0	0	0	0
2,120	2,160	161	123	96	70	44	18	0	0	0	0	0
2,160	2,200	167	129	100	74	48	22	0	0	0	0	0
2,200	2,240	173	135	104	78	52	26	0	0	0	0	0
2,240	2,280	179	141	108	82	56	30	4	0	0	0	0
2,280	2,320	185	147	112	86	60	34	8	0	0	0	0
2,320	2,360	191	153	116	90	64	38	12	0	0	0	0
2,360	2,400	197	159	120	94	68	42	16	0	0	0	0
2,400	2,440	203	165	126	98	72	46	20	0	0	0	0
2,440	2,480	209	171	132	102	76	50	24	0	0	0	0
2,480	2,520	215	177	138	106	80	54	28	3	0	0	0
2,520	2,560	221	183	144	110	84	58	32	7	0	0	0
2,560	2,600	227	189	150	114	88	62	36	11	0	0	0
2,600	2,640	233	195	156	118	92	66	40	15	0	0	0
2,640	2,680	239	201	162	123	96	70	44	19	0	0	0
2,680	2,720	245	207	168	129	100	74	48	23	0	0	0
2,720	2,760	251	213	174	135	104	78	52	27	1	0	0
2,760	2,800	257	219	180	141	108	82	56	31	5	0	0
2,800	2,840	263	225	186	147	112	86	60	35	9	0	0
2,840	2,880	269	231	192	153	116	90	64	39	13	0	0
2,880	2,920	275	237	198	159	120	94	68	43	17	0	0
2,920	2,960	281	243	204	165	126	98	72	47	21	0	0
2,960	3,000	287	249	210	171	132	102	76	51	25	0	0
3,000	3,040	293	255	216	177	138	106	80	55	29	3	0
3,040	3,080	299	261	222	183	144	110	84	59	33	7	0
3,080	3,120	305	267	228	189	150	114	88	63	37	11	0
3,120	3,160	311	273	234	195	156	118	92	67	41	15	0
3,160	3,200	317	279	240	201	162	124	96	71	45	19	0
3,200	3,240	323	285	246	207	168	130	100	75	49	23	0

MARRIED Persons—MONTHLY Payroll Period

(For Wages Paid Through December 2004)

If the wages are—		And the number of withholding allowances claimed is—										
At least	But less than	0	1	2	3	4	5	6	7	8	9	10
		The amount of income tax to be withheld is—										
$3,240	$3,280	$329	$291	$252	$213	$174	$136	$104	$79	$53	$27	$1
3,280	3,320	335	297	258	219	180	142	108	83	57	31	5
3,320	3,360	341	303	264	225	186	148	112	87	61	35	9
3,360	3,400	347	309	270	231	192	154	116	91	65	39	13
3,400	3,440	353	315	276	237	198	160	121	95	69	43	17
3,440	3,480	359	321	282	243	204	166	127	99	73	47	21
3,480	3,520	365	327	288	249	210	172	133	103	77	51	25
3,520	3,560	371	333	294	255	216	178	139	107	81	55	29
3,560	3,600	377	339	300	261	222	184	145	111	85	59	33
3,600	3,640	383	345	306	267	228	190	151	115	89	63	37
3,640	3,680	389	351	312	273	234	196	157	119	93	67	41
3,680	3,720	395	357	318	279	240	202	163	124	97	71	45
3,720	3,760	401	363	324	285	246	208	169	130	101	75	49
3,760	3,800	407	369	330	291	252	214	175	136	105	79	53
3,800	3,840	413	375	336	297	258	220	181	142	109	83	57
3,840	3,880	419	381	342	303	264	226	187	148	113	87	61
3,880	3,920	425	387	348	309	270	232	193	154	117	91	65
3,920	3,960	431	393	354	315	276	238	199	160	121	95	69
3,960	4,000	437	399	360	321	282	244	205	166	127	99	73
4,000	4,040	443	405	366	327	288	250	211	172	133	103	77
4,040	4,080	449	411	372	333	294	256	217	178	139	107	81
4,080	4,120	455	417	378	339	300	262	223	184	145	111	85
4,120	4,160	461	423	384	345	306	268	229	190	151	115	89
4,160	4,200	467	429	390	351	312	274	235	196	157	119	93
4,200	4,240	473	435	396	357	318	280	241	202	163	125	97
4,240	4,280	479	441	402	363	324	286	247	208	169	131	101
4,280	4,320	485	447	408	369	330	292	253	214	175	137	105
4,320	4,360	491	453	414	375	336	298	259	220	181	143	109
4,360	4,400	497	459	420	381	342	304	265	226	187	149	113
4,400	4,440	503	465	426	387	348	310	271	232	193	155	117
4,440	4,480	509	471	432	393	354	316	277	238	199	161	122
4,480	4,520	515	477	438	399	360	322	283	244	205	167	128
4,520	4,560	521	483	444	405	366	328	289	250	211	173	134
4,560	4,600	527	489	450	411	372	334	295	256	217	179	140
4,600	4,640	533	495	456	417	378	340	301	262	223	185	146
4,640	4,680	539	501	462	423	384	346	307	268	229	191	152
4,680	4,720	545	507	468	429	390	352	313	274	235	197	158
4,720	4,760	551	513	474	435	396	358	319	280	241	203	164
4,760	4,800	557	519	480	441	402	364	325	286	247	209	170
4,800	4,840	563	525	486	447	408	370	331	292	253	215	176
4,840	4,880	569	531	492	453	414	376	337	298	259	221	182
4,880	4,920	575	537	498	459	420	382	343	304	265	227	188
4,920	4,960	581	543	504	465	426	388	349	310	271	233	194
4,960	5,000	587	549	510	471	432	394	355	316	277	239	200
5,000	5,040	593	555	516	477	438	400	361	322	283	245	206
5,040	5,080	599	561	522	483	444	406	367	328	289	251	212
5,080	5,120	605	567	528	489	450	412	373	334	295	257	218
5,120	5,160	611	573	534	495	456	418	379	340	301	263	224
5,160	5,200	617	579	540	501	462	424	385	346	307	269	230
5,200	5,240	623	585	546	507	468	430	391	352	313	275	236
5,240	5,280	629	591	552	513	474	436	397	358	319	281	242
5,280	5,320	635	597	558	519	480	442	403	364	325	287	248
5,320	5,360	641	603	564	525	486	448	409	370	331	293	254
5,360	5,400	647	609	570	531	492	454	415	376	337	299	260
5,400	5,440	656	615	576	537	498	460	421	382	343	305	266
5,440	5,480	666	621	582	543	504	466	427	388	349	311	272
5,480	5,520	676	627	588	549	510	472	433	394	355	317	278
5,520	5,560	686	633	594	555	516	478	439	400	361	323	284
5,560	5,600	696	639	600	561	522	484	445	406	367	329	290
5,600	5,640	706	645	606	567	528	490	451	412	373	335	296
5,640	5,680	716	651	612	573	534	496	457	418	379	341	302
5,680	5,720	726	661	618	579	540	502	463	424	385	347	308
5,720	5,760	736	671	624	585	546	508	469	430	391	353	314
5,760	5,800	746	681	630	591	552	514	475	436	397	359	320
5,800	5,840	756	691	636	597	558	520	481	442	403	365	326
5,840	5,880	766	701	642	603	564	526	487	448	409	371	332

$5,880 and over   Use Table 4(b) for a **MARRIED person** on page 3. Also see the instructions on page 2.

Unit 4

Applications Evaluation

Last Name   First Name

Refer to completed Applications 4-1 through 4-6 to answer the following questions. The total point value of all the questions for each application as well as the point value of each individual question is indicated by the numbers in parentheses. Leave the Points Earned column blank. Your teacher will complete it.

Application 4-1

Points Earned

Calculate Cash Drawer Funds (4) (2 each)

What was the combined amount of coins in all three cash drawer counts? _____

of 4

What was the combined amount of bills in all three cash drawer counts? _____

Application 4-2

Prepare Petty Cash Record (10) (Value beside each)

of 10

For the month, what was the total amount spent for

Office Expense	(1) _____	Supplies Expense	(1)_____
Delivery Expense	(1) _____	Warehouse Expense	(1)_____
Postage Expense	(1) _____	Miscellaneous Expense	(1)_____

What was the total amount spent for all items from 3/1 to 3/15 (including 3/15)? (2)_____

What was the total amount spent for all items from 3/16 to 3/31 (including 3/31)? (2)_____

Application 4-3

Balance Ledger Accounts (14) (1 each)

of 14

What was the balance of Account No. 1139 on March 1? _____

What was the balance of Account No. 2045 on March 15? _____

What was the balance of Account No. 3705 on February 15? _____

What was the balance of Account No. 6390 on February 1? _____

What was the balance of Account No. 10348 on March 3? _____

What was the balance of Account No. 11824 on March 20? _____

What was the balance of Account No. 12037 on March 25? _____

What was the balance of Account No. 16492 on February 16? _____

What was the balance of Account No. 16720 on March 30? _____

What was the balance of Account No. 17730 on March 15? _____

What was the balance of Account No. 18829 on March 18? _____

What was the balance of Account No. 20104 on March 2? _____

What was the balance of Account No. 20390 on March 6? _____

What was the balance of Account No. 20395 on March 14? _____

Application 4-4

Prepare Biweekly Payroll Record (23) (Value beside each)

What was the total amount deducted in FICA taxes for all married employees? (4)_____

What was the total amount deducted in federal income taxes for all single employees? (4)_____

What was the total amount deducted in state income taxes for all married employees? (4)_____

What was the total credit union amount deducted for all employees? (1)_____

What was the total amount of net earnings for all married employees? (4)_____

What was the difference between the federal income taxes paid by all married employees and the federal income taxes paid by all single employees? (3)_____

What was the difference between the state income taxes paid by all married employees and the state income taxes paid by all single employees? (3)_____

Application 4-5

Calculate Weekly Payroll (18) (Value beside each)

What was the total amount of net pay for all married employees? (3)_____

What was the total amount deducted in federal and state income taxes for all married employees? (4)_____

What was the total amount deducted in federal, state, and FICA taxes for all employees? (2)_____

What was the total amount of all deductions for all single employees? (4)_____

What was the total amount of net pay for all employees with one exemption? (2)_____

What was the difference between the total deductions for all married employees and the total deductions for all single employees? (3)_____

Application 4-6

Determine Salary Plus Commission Payroll (31) (Value beside each)

What was the total dues, charities, and credit union amount deducted for all single employees? (5)_____

What was the total amount deducted in federal income taxes for all married employees? (3)_____

What was the total amount deducted in state income taxes for all employees with one dependent? (3)_____

What was the total amount of commissions earned by all employees earning a salary of at least $1,700 but less than $1,900? (3)_____

What was the total amount of commissions earned by all employees earning a salary of $1,900 or more? (3)_____

What was the total amount of gross earnings for all married employees? (2)_____

What was the total amount of commissions earned by all single employees? (2)_____

What was the total amount of net earnings for all employees with one dependent? (2)_____

What was the total amount of salary for all employees with two or more dependents? (2)_____

What was the difference between the FICA taxes paid by all married employees and the FICA taxes paid by all single employees? (2)_____

What was the difference between the federal income taxes paid by all married employees and the federal income taxes paid by all single employees? (2)_____

What was the difference between the state income taxes paid by all married employees and the state income taxes paid by all single employees? (2)_____

Grading Scale

A = 100–94 points
B = 93–86 points
C = 85–78 points
D = 77–70 points

Total Points Earned of 100 _____

Unit 4 Applications Evaluation Grade _____